What If?

How to overcome
Worry, *Fear*, and *Anxiety*
and turn them into
Peace, *Faith*, and *Hope*.

By Author

John Stone

Table of Contents

Chapter One

Introduction

In this book, I'm going to talk to you about words and the power they have in the lives of believers. We will dive into the biblical principles surrounding this subject and look into how our thoughts can affect our lives.

I have read many books about the power of our words and the power of our thoughts. I noticed in almost all of them that they tend to use 100-200 pages to discuss the one primary topic and present it to you repeatedly in dozens of different ways.

While I enjoy that style of writing, I decided that I wanted to write this book differently. I tried to make it more diverse. I didn't want to focus on one primary topic and leave it at that. I wanted to give you many different subjects to think about.

This is why I decided to begin the next chapter with a little bit of background information about our spiritual adversary. Then, in the third chapter, I move on to a discussion about the enemy's intentions. I used the fourth, fifth, and sixth chapters to discuss how the devil does what he does. It isn't until the seventh chapter that I begin to get into this book's core topic. After that, I use the eighth, ninth, and tenth chapters to teach about faith, as well as the power of our thoughts and words.

I want to make this book a tool for those who struggle with various types of difficulties and trials in their lives, which would be every one of us.

Humans are multi-faceted beings. Not only are we physical creatures, but we are spiritual creatures as well. It is so easy to get caught up in the physical aspect of our lives. In doing so, we tend to ignore the spiritual part of ourselves. It's easy to understand how this can happen and become so prevalent in the lives of believers. With the constant demands life places on us, it's no wonder that we can so easily forget to care for our spiritual selves.

What we will do here is take time out of our busy schedules to focus on our spiritual health. Doing so will provide us with the endurance we need to run the race that is before us.

Before we discuss the power of our words and thoughts in great depth and how Satan tries to use them against us, we will explore many other tactics that the enemy uses to harm us. I believe that if we are going to use some of the greatest tools God has given us, which are our thoughts and our words, we must first learn how Satan tries to use these same life-giving tools to accomplish his purpose.

We must first learn as much as we can about the enemy. We need to know who it is we are fighting. We need to know what his intentions are and what he hopes to accomplish. We also need to understand how the enemy fights. If we can learn how the enemy fights, we will be better prepared to defend ourselves.

Think back to World War II. On December 7th, 1941, the Japanese initiated their sneak attack against the United States. In this attack, there were 2,403 people killed and 1,178 wounded.

Can you imagine how this could have turned out if the United States had known in advance of the enemy's plan to attack? I can imagine the U.S. would have had all of its battleships and warplanes prepared and ready to defend against the enemy. There would have been a lot fewer casualties in our country had our nation been prepared. Simply knowing who their enemy was, knowing their strategies, and knowing their fighting tactics could have saved thousands of lives.

The United States didn't have the advantage of knowing in advance of the enemy's plan to attack. As believers, we don't have that same excuse when it comes to defending ourselves against our greatest adversary. We have everything we need at our fingertips. All we have to do is turn the pages in the most fabulous book ever written, the Bible.

Within the pages of the Bible lays the battle plan. There's step by step instructions on how to defeat the enemy. As long as we invest the time and are willing to go through a spiritual boot camp, I believe we can prepare ourselves to face every challenge that comes our way. After all, Jesus told us we would have troubles in this world (John 16:33). It should not come as a surprise to believers that we will indeed face many struggles. What is important to remember is that we will not face them alone.

Jesus also said in John 16:33 that we do not need to worry because He has faced all of the troubles of this world and has overcome them all.

I know what you're thinking. It's easy for Him to tell us not to worry. It's easy for Him to overcome all of His difficulties. After all, He is the Son of God. While it is true, He is the Son of God, it is also true that He was a human being, just like the rest of us. He experienced life just as we have experienced it. He felt the pain as the soldiers viciously hammered the nails into his wrists, no different than any other man would. When the soldiers ridiculed Him and placed a crown made of thorns on His head, the thorns punctured His skin, causing blood to drip down His face. He also felt the agony as the Roman soldiers violently whipped Him, leaving Him just a few lashes away from death.

Jesus experienced every human emotion that we have experienced. He endured troubles more significant than a lot of us have ever encountered. Because He has been through all of these things, He can speak from experience when He said, "In this world, you will have trouble. But take heart! I have overcome the world." He did indeed overcome the world by rising from the grave on the third day.

Because of all He has done, we can rest assured knowing that we too can overcome the troubles of this world. We know this because the Bible tells us in 1 John 4:4 that *He who is in me is greater than the one who is in the world.* He has already conquered the world through His death and resurrection. Because we have accepted Him as our Lord and Savior, his spirit lives within us. With the Word of God living in us, there isn't anything we can't overcome!

Chapter Two

Where the fight is coming from

Ephesians 6:12
For our struggle is not against flesh and blood, but against the rulers, against the authorities, against the powers of this dark world and against the spiritual forces of evil in the heavenly realms.

The Bible tells us that our lives here on this earth go way beyond physical existence. It tells us that the battles we face are not from a natural source. The battles that try to overtake us come from the spiritual realm. Everything that happens here on earth has a spiritual connection to it. We tend to look at all the adversities in our life and believe that we are alone in our battles. This isn't true. We have spiritual forces working behind the scenes in our lives every day. We can't see it with our eyes. We can't hear the battle cries with our ears, but we can be sure there is a battle raging on for our souls.

The forces of darkness are working against us. The enemy is working tirelessly to capture our souls. While we know this is true, what we may not understand is how the forces of darkness operate. In other words, what is the enemy's battle plan? Do we know the tactics Satan uses against us? Would we recognize an attack from the enemy when it's taking place? Most of us could be in the middle of the battle of Armageddon and not even realize it is happening.

We know that Satan has waged war against God since the beginning of time. And since then, he has desired to overtake the world.

It all started in chapter three of the book of Genesis. We can see here that some of Satan's greatest strategies include using deception, lies, and temptation to try to capture our souls. These are some of the most common weapons he uses in this war that he has waged against us.

I believe that knowing the real source of our troubles can allow us to resolve them more effectively. Let's think about a hypothetical scenario where the faucet in your kitchen is leaking. You want to fix it, but where do you begin? You wouldn't go into the bathroom and start taking apart the pipes behind the toilet, would you? Of course not. Any logical person would begin by taking their toolkit to the pipes underneath the kitchen sink.

What if you fell and injured your knee? Let's say that you walk, or should I say, limp, into your doctor's office. You tell him your knee hurts. Would you expect the doctor to take an x-ray of your elbow? Of course not. If he did, you would probably wobble out of his office as fast as you could. You wouldn't get any results if your doctor wasn't looking in the right place.

Knowing the source of the problem is the best way to begin your fight against it. And the origin of life's battles is in the heavenly realms, against the spiritual forces of evil. The spiritual realm is where we must focus our efforts. This is where the conflict begins, and this is where we must fight if we hope to win.

Chapter Three

The Enemy's intention

John 10:10

The thief comes only to steal and kill and destroy; I have come that they may have life, and have it to the full.

1st Peter 5:8-11

Be alert and of sober mind. Your enemy, the devil, prowls around like a roaring lion looking for someone to devour. Resist him, standing firm in the faith, because you know that the family of believers throughout the world is undergoing the same kind of sufferings.

It's no secret what Satan's intentions are. It's obvious what he wants. It says in the Gospel of John that his purpose is to steal, kill, and destroy. His only desire is to inflict pain, destruction, and suffering. He wishes only to create chaos, confusion, and unrest.

He does all these things for a reason. That reason is to capture our souls. He knows if he steals our hope that we might give up on God. He knows that if he kills our faith, that we will inevitably surrender to fear. He knows that if he can destroy the things that connect us to God, that our souls will be left in his control, to do with as he pleases.

We know there are forces in the spiritual realm fighting for our souls. What we can sometimes forget to realize is that the One working for us is greater than the one who is working against us. (1 John 4:4)

While we know why Satan is here, do we also know why God sent Jesus? In the same scripture that reveals to us Satan's intentions, we also learn what Jesus' plans are. Jesus said, "I have come that they may have life, and have it to the full." He told us His intention in a clear and precise manner. He didn't use a parable or a metaphor. He told us He came here to be with us so that through Him, we can live a life of victory.

Living our lives through Him can provide us with the peace, faith, and hope that we need to overcome the enemy's constant and ferocious attacks. We must also remember that He intends to give us the ability to live life here on earth to the fullest and live our eternity to the fullest.

In 1st Peter 5:8-11, the Bible tells us that Satan prowls the earth like a roaring lion, looking for those that he can devour. This scripture also warns us to be alert and aware. It tells us to stand firm in the faith. Right here, in these three verses of the book of 1st Peter, the Bible shares with us everything we need to do to avoid becoming the lion's lunch.

We need to be aware of the enemy's tactics, and we need to stand firm in our faith. How do we do these things? We need to study God's word.

Romans 10:17 says that faith comes by hearing the word. God has given us everything we need to live a blessed and victorious life here on earth. We can find every word of wisdom and every promise of His in the Bible.

We must read His word every day, feeding off of it, renewing our minds, and nourishing our souls. It's no different than the food we consume each day. We need to eat to nourish our bodies. Imagine how weak our bodies would become if we didn't consume our daily nutritional requirements?

It's the same with our spirit. We need to consume our spiritual food daily so we can maintain our spiritual strength. You wouldn't go days without eating, would you? Then why would you go days without consuming God's word?

Fortunately for us, just as there are many different kinds of foods to choose from, there are also many different ways to obtain our spiritual nourishment. First, there are your local churches that can feed your soul through worship services on Sundays and through Bible study classes that most churches offer throughout the week. Then you have your tv preachers. There are also resources like YouTube, where you can find thousands of sermons from hundreds of preachers worldwide. So, whether you like to stay home and cook (tv preachers) or go out to dinner (church), there are always various ways to find the spiritual food you need.

Because there are so many ways to access the word of God, there isn't any excuse not to do so. You can listen to a preacher in your car on the way to work or listen to an audio version of the Bible on your morning walk. The word of God is all around us.

We must understand that we are at war. Because of this, we must be diligent in our preparedness. When you were in school and had final exams coming up, you would prepare for them, wouldn't you? You would spend hours studying and getting ready for the tests. Why did you do this? Because you knew that if you didn't prepare for the tests, you would likely fail. Why would we want to fail the most significant test of all?

I've always believed in this philosophy: Do your best and trust God for the rest. It's simple. Use the resources God has given you. Having a strong foundation in God's word will provide you with the support you need when the enemy attacks.

Chapter Four

Tactics of The Enemy: Deception

One of the greatest weapons Satan has to use against us is the power of deception.

It says in John 8:44 that Satan is the father of lies.

He fools us into believing that we are facing battles against each other. He convinces us that all of our life's difficulties are simply a matter of chance. He makes us believe that all we can do is deal with the hand that life has dealt us. He makes it appear as though we are fighting all of our battles in the natural world. When we believe these lies, we fail to realize that the supernatural realm is where we should fight our battles.

The devil is distracting us by having us take our focus away from the supernatural and have us re-direct our focus onto the natural. We are then blinding ourselves to God's presence and His power.

Imagine what life could be like if we looked at it through God's eyes? We would never see defeat. We would never feel hopeless. We would never surrender to the fear that comes with believing that we must fight all of life's battles alone. God is here for us. He told us He would never leave us, and He will never forsake us. (Deuteronomy 31:6)

If we face an illness, we are conditioned to believe that doctors and medicine are the only sources of relief. I can't deny that medical science can do some amazing things. And I know that God sometimes works through these channels. However, we must understand there are times when we can't fight the battle with only our physical strength.

Science doesn't always have a solution to every one of life's problems. There are times when medicine and surgeries can't heal an illness or disease. There are times when we need to look beyond the natural realm and look to God for the things we can't do within our strength alone. When we look to God for these things, we are fighting against the lies of the enemy. His lies try to keep us in bondage to a world that offers us nothing and takes us away from a God that can provide us with everything.

The devil will bring difficulties and strife into our marriage and then try to deceive us into believing that our spouse is the source of the problem. Whether it's the husband spending too much on the credit cards or the wife working too much overtime, he will try to convince us that these things are worth fighting over. He tells you that it's ok to be resentful towards your partner because of these behaviors. Once he has done this, he has become successful in infiltrating your marriage. He has planted a seed, and if it grows roots, it will continue to spread and possibly tear apart your relationship.

When friends are not there for you when you need them the most, or when a family member talks about you behind your back, don't let that bother you. Those are just distractions. Or when colleagues lie about you to the boss, don't pay any attention. It's just a distraction.

The devil will try to manipulate the people around you to distract you. He will deceive you into believing that people have influence over your life. The truth is, you are the only one that can choose who influences your life. If you allow the devil to deceive you into believing that these people can make you happy or unhappy, then guess what, they will.

We need to realize that our happiness, peace, and joy come from only one source: from God.

Seriously, if someone lies about you, do you think the lie is going to change how God perceives you? Do you think God is going to believe the lie? No. He's not. His perception cannot be changed by what people believe about you. He will always love you and be there for you no matter what others may say about you. The truth so many of us fail to recognize is that what people think about us doesn't matter.

Ultimately, the devil will try to direct your focus away from God and towards the things of this world. By doing so, he is taking our attention away from the only real hope we have. God is our source of strength. He is the only one that can provide us with all we are searching for in this life.

Let's take a closer look at biblical references to deception and the power it has to ruin us.

Genesis 3:1-7

Now the serpent was craftier than any of the wild animals the Lord God had made. He said to the woman, "Did God really say, 'You must not eat from any tree in the garden'?"

The woman said to the serpent, "We may eat fruit from the trees in the garden, but God did say, 'You must not eat fruit from the tree that is in the middle of the garden, and you must not touch it, or you will die.'"

"You will not certainly die," the serpent said to the woman. "For God knows that when you eat from it, your eyes will be opened, and you will be like God, knowing good and evil."

When the woman saw that the fruit of the tree was good for food and pleasing to the eye, and also desirable for gaining wisdom, she took some and ate it. She also gave some to her husband, who was with her, and he ate it. Then the eyes of both of them were opened, and they realized they were naked; so they sewed fig leaves together and made coverings for themselves.

In this scripture from the book of Genesis, we can see how the devil tried to deceive Eve. First, he questioned Eve's understanding of God's instruction. In the inquiry that he made to Eve, he misquoted God.

He changed the actual words that God had spoken to her. Rather than ask Eve if God told her not to eat from this one tree, he asked, "Did God tell you not to eat from any of the trees in the garden?" He put words into God's mouth that He never said. He knew what God said. But he changed it, so Eve would have to think, *Did God really say not to eat from any of the trees, or just this one?* He's tried to create self-doubt. "Surely Eve, you must have misunderstood Him," is what he was asking her.

Eve then responded with, "We may eat fruit from the trees in the garden, but God did say, 'You must not eat fruit from the tree that is in the middle of the garden, and you must not touch it, or you will die.'" After this response, Satan realized that his effort to create self-doubt in Eve's mind didn't succeed. She corrected him and told him God's actual words. When the devil heard this, he then proceeded to challenge God by calling Him a liar. Can you believe that? The master of all lies called God a liar. He told Eve that she wouldn't die if she ate the forbidden fruit.

He went on to say to her, "For God knows that when you eat from it, your eyes will be opened, and you will be like God, knowing good and evil." Now this part was correct. Here, you see how the enemy takes some truth, mixes it with lies, packages it up with a little temptation, and presents it to us. Now, this was very skillful on his part. By adding some truth to it, he gives her the illusion that his entire statement is true. Wow. That's very slick. Then add the part about her ability to become like God. That was very tempting. I mean, who wouldn't be tempted by that offer. So, you can see how easy it was for her to give in to the lies and temptation.

Things like this happen to us every day. And just like Eve, we don't even realize it's happening most of the time. People can be fooled so easily into believing things that aren't real.

For example, consider the widespread belief that the world is flat. Many years ago, someone came up with the theory that the world was flat. Apparently, this person told another person, and that person told another person, and so on. Eventually, a vast majority of people on this earth believed that it was flat.

The bottom line is that the human mind can be persuaded to believe whatever it wants to believe. If a person can convince another person that the world is flat, how much easier do you think it is for the prince of darkness to persuade us that his lies are real? Let's move on.

Genesis 3:12-13
The man replied, "It was the woman you gave me who gave me the fruit, and I ate it." Then the Lord God asked the woman, "What have you done?" "The serpent deceived me," she replied. "That's why I ate it."

In this scripture, we can see how Adam blamed Eve for his part in the situation. He told God, "It was the women You gave me who made me eat the fruit." It's as if he was saying, "God, it's your fault. You made her, and she made me do it."

As we can see here in this scripture, the devil was working behind the scenes to influence Adam to blame Eve and then blame God. Now that's a pretty bold thing to do. Even I've been around long enough to know not to do something as foolish as that. But I suppose that in Adam's defense, it was his first day on the job.

Let's continue by looking at this next scripture.

Colossians 2:8

Be careful that no one takes you captive through philosophy and empty deceit based on human tradition, based on the elemental forces of the world, and not based on Christ.

This Bible verse warns us not to fall victim to the lies of the enemy. There are lies all around us. We've all been lied to, whether it's a car salesman who lies to us or a loved one who betrays us with deception. We have all experienced this in our lives.

There are also a lot of times when we are the ones telling the lies. Sometimes we lie to ourselves, and sometimes we lie to others.

The devil is the master of all lies. He can persuade us to lie to ourselves and convince us that the lies we tell ourselves are real. Lies like, "I'm not good enough," or, "I don't deserve anything good in my life," or, "I will never see God's blessings in my life." These are just a few of the lies that we tell ourselves every day. Whether we tell ourselves these lies, or whether it's someone else telling us, we hear them so often that they become engraved in our hearts.

Whether we realize it or not, we are all continually listening to the words that have been carved into our hearts. This is the form of influence Satan uses to hold us down. It keeps us from the power we have through God's Word. Let's not stop here. Let's move on to this scripture.

2 Timothy 3:13-14

But evil people and impostors will go from bad to worse as they deceive others and are themselves deceived. But as for you, continue in what you have learned and found to be true, because you know from whom you learned it.

This scripture once again teaches us that the devil uses people to spread his lies and deception. Now while it references evil people, don't believe for a moment that decent people aren't susceptible to the same tactics of the enemy. We all have fallen victim to the lies of the enemy at some time in our lives. And we have all been the ones to spread them as well. I'm not trying to judge with my comments here. I'm merely trying to point out the fact that if we are not careful, we too can be consumed by the lion.

This scripture tells us how we can avoid the traps the enemy has laid out for us. It tells us to continue using what we have learned and know to be true.

How do we learn the truth? By reading the Bible.

Now I'm not going to ignore the fact that if this book I'm writing were to fall into the hands of a non-believer, and I hope it does, they would most likely ask, "How do I know the Bible is the truth?" My answer to this is simple. We can believe that the Bible is the truth of God by having faith that it is.

How can a non-believer have faith that a book written thousands of years ago can be true? The answer lies within the book.

Romans 10:17 says: *Consequently, faith comes from hearing the message, and the message is heard through the word about Christ.* Right here, it tells us that we must hear the word of God if we are to have faith. We must read the Bible to build the faith that it takes to believe in its truth. This scripture tells us we need to hear the message and that we can hear the message through the word about Christ. It tells us exactly where to look. If a non-believer wants to honestly know how he or she can understand if the Bible is the real word of God, the only way to find out is to read it. If you read it, you will be able to hear the message that is written throughout the pages of the Bible. But the only way you will hear it is if you choose to listen. What I mean by this is that reading the Bible isn't enough. There is a message within it, but you must choose to listen to it.

It's like when someone leaves you a voicemail on your phone. You have to choose to press a button to play the message. Then you have to decide to listen to it. The message is there, but you will never hear it unless you choose to listen to it. The bible is the same. You must choose to listen to it. Listening to it is more than just reading it.

If your friend left you a voicemail, and you pressed the button and listened to it, would you believe that your friend is the one who sent it? Or, would you doubt he or she sent it? Would you think that the message appeared on your phone without anyone sending it? I think that would be foolish to believe. Believing the Bible is a message that was sent without anyone sending it would be just as silly.

Being the analytical thinker that I am, I will go one step forward and presume that a non-believer would argue, how do I know the Bible came from God and not the men who wrote it? I would answer this question with a question. Why would any of the authors have any reason to lie? Do you think the devil is deceiving them into telling the world that there is a God when there isn't? That's probably the last thing the devil would want you to believe. And let's face it, if there was no God, then it's reasonable to assume the devil isn't real either. So, if there were no God, then there wouldn't be a devil to spread lies about there being a God. So, therefore, this theory defeats itself.

Someone might believe that the bible is a bunch of make-believe stories intended to be used to control people into behaving a certain way. After all, we tell our children there's a chubby man in a red suit that flies all around the world, delivering millions of toys to children in the period of just one single night. We then tell our kids he flies a sled that doesn't have an engine and has reindeer pulling it through the star-filled night sky. The reason we tell them this fairytale is so we can get them to behave by telling them that if they don't, Santa won't bring them any presents for Christmas. We go so far as to threaten to call Santa to tell him about the naughty things our children are doing. We ask Santa to put them on the naughty list and give them a lump of coal in their stocking rather than toys.

So yes, people tell make-believe stories so they can control someone else through fear. My question to you is, why would the authors of the Bible have any desire to control us? Why would they risk their lives to do so? The stories they were telling were not popular amongst the authority at the time. Sharing these stories of a God who loves us so much that He would give His only Son for us, were stories that would likely have gotten them killed. And according to scripture, many of them were killed.

In biblical times, many people believed in false gods. If you challenged the authority's belief system and told them the gods they believed in weren't real and that there was only one true living God, you would likely pay the price for it.

Our government believes that driving too fast on our roads could be dangerous. Our politicians have written laws allowing them to dictate how fast we can drive. I have challenged that belief system many times. Every time I did, I paid the price (I've been issued many tickets throughout the years).

It was the same when the followers of Christ challenged the authority's belief system thousands of years ago. The only difference is, their fine was more severe than mine.

While I know the Bible could be just a series of entertaining stories, a person must first turn the pages, one by one, to see for themselves. I could continue with this subject for several more chapters, but instead, if you are a non-believer reading this book, I ask you to keep turning the pages, not just the pages of this book, but also the pages of the Bible. See where it takes you. Listen to see if you can hear the message being spoken. Let's move on.

Corinthians 15:33
Do not be deceived: "Bad company ruins good morals."

Satan can use deception in many different ways. As Corinthians 15: 33 teaches us, we can be deceived into believing that being in the company of bad people is not going to corrupt us. This belief is not valid. How many times have I been in the company of someone that has persuaded me into doing something I didn't want to do? How about you? Have you not been subject to peer pressure? Have you ever heard the phrase; *a chain is only as strong as its weakest link?* All it takes is one weak link to break the chain.

1 John 1:8

If we say that we do not have any sin, we are deceiving ourselves, and we're not true to ourselves.

This is one of the devil's best strategies. He leads us to believe that we are spiritually *Ok*. He convinces some of us that because we go to church and pay our tithes, we will surely go to heaven when we die.

Let me ask this. If the rapture were to happen today, how many of us would be left behind? Most of us believe that the churches would be empty and the prisons would remain full at the moment of the rapture. If you believe this, then you are deceived. It doesn't matter if we go to church. It doesn't even matter if we are in prison. What matters is what's on the inside of us. Our heart is what is going to lead us to heaven or hell. The sin that led a man to prison can be forgiven if he repents. It's no different than the man on the cross next to Jesus, who gave his life to the Lord during the last hours of his life. Jesus told him he would be in paradise with him on that day.

We must be careful not to deceive ourselves into believing that we are ok. Remember, the scripture says that Satan is scouring the earth to see who he may devour. It doesn't say he scoured the earth, got tired, and gave up. No, it says that he scours the earth. It's written in the present tense, not the past tense. What this means is that he is still roaming the earth and consuming souls.

The fight doesn't end until our very last breath is taken. Believe it or not, some battles can be won or lost in the very final moments of our lives, just like a basketball team that makes that last-second shot just before the time runs out on the clock. The game is tied. Moments before the buzzer sounds, their star player shoots the ball right into the net. Just moments before, it seemed like they weren't going to win. But at the very last moment, they received the victory.

While winning at the end is possible, the one difference between a basketball game and life is that in life, we never honestly know how much time we have left on the clock.

Corinthians 6:9-11

Don't you know that the unrighteous will not inherit God's kingdom? Do not be deceived: No sexually immoral people, idolaters, adulterers, or anyone practicing homosexuality, no thieves, greedy people, drunkards, verbally abusive people, or swindlers will inherit God's kingdom. And some of you used to be like this. But you were washed, you were sanctified, you were justified in the name of the Lord Jesus Christ and by the Spirit of our God.

Here we go again. This scripture warns us that deception can steal our souls. We all think we have plenty of time. Let me have fun now, and I'll say I'm sorry later. Right? Have you ever felt like this in life?

This kind of thinking leads people to engage in these sins. People think to themselves, I'll play now and pay later. They believe that all they need to do is say I'm sorry. That's a small price to pay for all of this fun, isn't it? This plan should work, right?

Actually, that's not how it works. We can't forget that God can see inside our hearts. He knows our intentions, and if our apologies are sincere. We can't deceive God. This is a truth that we must understand.

As it describes in Corinthians 6: 9-11, people that do these sinful things will not enter the kingdom of God. However, take note of the fact that it is written in the present tense. This means that if we died while in the midst of these sins, we risk losing the kingdom of God. However, it goes on to say that some of us used to be like those people who do those sinful things. It tells us that we were washed, sanctified, and justified through the blood of Jesus Christ. It assures us that we are saved once we repent and accept Jesus as our savior.

So, as we have seen here in these scriptures, there are countless ways in which Satan uses deception to carry out his mission to steal, kill, and destroy. Sometimes he uses people to distract us, and sometimes he deceives us into believing that we are spiritually ok when we might not be. Either way, we know that he is coming after us. We should prepare ourselves.

Chapter Five

Tactics of the Enemy: Temptation

Temptation is another one of the greatest weapons that Satan has in his arsenal. He even used temptation as a weapon in his attempt to defeat Jesus. This goes to show that every one of us is susceptible to this tactic. Let's begin this chapter by discussing several biblical scriptures referencing temptation and how the devil uses it to try to capture our souls. Let's look at Jesus' experience in Matthew 4:1-11.

Matthew 4:1-11
Then Jesus was led by the Spirit into the wilderness to be tempted by the devil. After fasting forty days and forty nights, he was hungry. The tempter came to him and said, "If you are the Son of God, tell these stones to become bread." Jesus answered, "It is written: 'Man shall not live on bread alone, but on every word that comes from the mouth of God." Then the devil took him to the holy city and had him stand on the highest point of the temple. "If you are the Son of God," he said, "throw yourself down. For it is written:

"'He will command his angels concerning you, and they will lift you up in their hands so that you will not strike your foot against a stone."

Jesus answered him, "It is also written: 'Do not put the Lord your God to the test.'" Again, the devil took him to a very high mountain and showed him all the kingdoms of the world and their splendor. "All this I will give you," he said, "if you will bow down and worship me." Jesus said to him, "Away from me, Satan! For it is written: 'Worship the Lord your God, and serve him only.'" Then the devil left him, and angels came and attended him.

In these scriptures, we can see that the Son of God wasn't exempt from the enemy's attacks. Satan went so far as to use scripture in his effort to tempt Jesus into sin. How did Jesus respond? He responded as any well-prepared believer would. He used the word of His Father to resist the enemy.

Satan will use every weapon in his arsenal to wreak havoc on our lives. If we are not careful, he will devour us. We must be in constant preparation for his attacks. Here is another scripture that we must look at when exploring the topic of temptation:

James 1:13-18

When tempted, no one should say, "God is tempting me." For God cannot be tempted by evil, nor does he tempt anyone; but each person is tempted when they are dragged away by their own evil desire and enticed.

Then, after desire has conceived, it gives birth to sin; and sin, when it is full-grown, gives birth to death.

This is a very powerful scripture. It teaches us a lot about temptation. It shows us that if we surrender to it, it can lead us to death. However, it isn't talking only about physical death. It is also talking about spiritual death.

One of the first things I noticed about this scripture was that God could not be tempted by evil. But wait a minute. Didn't we read earlier in the Gospel of Matthew that Satan tempted Christ? Yes, we did. In Mathew 4:1-11, we read about how Satan *tried* to tempt Jesus many times.

While Jesus was fasting, Satan tried to persuade Him to turn a stone into bread. Did Jesus do it? No, He didn't. Why? For many reasons. One reason was that Jesus had a purpose for what He was doing.

Fasting is a religious tradition that many different faiths practice in order to build up a resistance to the temptations of the flesh. Gluttony is one of the most common habits people struggle with. Imagine if we could control our urges to over-consume some of the most tempting culinary treats around us. I don't know about you, but rarely am I able to drive past a fast food restaurant without stopping for a delicious mouth-watering burger and some golden crispy fries. While I'm there, why not enjoy a large milkshake? What's the harm in that? It's not like I'm craving drugs, cigarettes, or anything harmful. It's just food, right?

Well, the answer to that is- no. Fasting is about more than just food.

One's ability to control themselves and resist temptation must be developed over time, through training. We must build up the strength we need to withstand some of the greater temptations that this world presents us. Jesus was fasting for a purpose. That purpose was to build strength.

Let's look at the gospel of Luke next.

Luke 16:10
Whoever can be trusted with very little can also be trusted with much, and whoever is dishonest with very little will also be dishonest with much.

Here in the Gospel of Luke, the word of God tells us that it is in the little things that our strength is made whole. Once we perfect our strength in the smaller things, then we will eventually be able to control our ability to resist the temptation for the more harmful things in life.

It's kind of like a bodybuilder's training program. Think of someone like Arnold Schwarzenegger. He is one of the best professional bodybuilders of all time. When he first started in the sport, do you think he could pick up a 500-hundred-pound barbell? No, of course not. Like every other person who is just beginning in the sport, he had to start with a much smaller amount of weight. He started with maybe a hundred or two hundred pounds. Then after that, he slowly worked his way up to five or six hundred pounds.

The average person doesn't decide to go to a gym for the first time in ten years and then lift a five-hundred-pound barbell above their head. I know if I tried to do that, I would probably hurt myself. There's no way I could have enough strength to lift that much weight unless I first started with something less significant. It would take time to build up enough strength to compete with a bodybuilding champ like Arnold.

Let's go back to Matthew 4:1-11. After Satan tried to persuade Jesus to turn a stone into bread, he then tried to tempt Jesus into testing the word of His Father. He told Jesus to leap off of the mountaintop and suggested He trust God to save Him.

I don't know about you, but that's a challenge I would never have accepted. That would have been an enormous leap of faith. However, for Jesus, this challenge that was made to Him would not have been a test.

A test is something that is done to measure one's abilities. It challenges an individual to see if they are capable of passing the test. Jesus had no reason to test the ability He already knew He had. After all, the man walked on water. He healed the sick and brought the dead back to life. Would He need to test the power of God? Of course not.

The Gospel of Mathew describes how Satan tried to tempt Jesus by offering Him power over all the kingdoms of the earth. I thought this offer was quite interesting. I look at this scripture and compare it to Christmas shopping. We all have one friend or family member that has it all. They have a beautiful house, a nice car, and every other materialistic thing one could desire. And if there was something they didn't have, they certainly could obtain it on their own.

So, what gift do you get someone who has everything? What can you offer them that they don't already have? Would you offer to give them the keys to their car? Would you offer to provide them with the keys to their own house? Of course not. You can't give someone something that is already theirs. I would laugh if a family member took my keys off the table and handed them to me, and said, "I got you a house for Christmas." I would remind them that this house already belongs to me. You can't offer me something that is already mine. This is precisely what Satan did. He offered Jesus authority over the world. How funny is that? Jesus already has power over all of creation. Satan hadn't offered Him anything He didn't already have.

So, what did Jesus do? He resisted every attempt the enemy made to lure Him into temptation. How did He do it? With the Word of God. He quoted scriptures and used the Word of God to resist the adversary. This scripture proves there is indeed power in the Word of God. It is like a sword and shield to those who have it living inside their soul.

Let's go back to the place in James 1:13-18, where it states that God can't be tempted. We just finished discussing how Satan tried to tempt Jesus. How is it then that God cannot be tempted? If we look further into James 1:13-18, we read that each person is tempted when they *are dragged away by their own evil desire and enticed.*

First of all, Jesus never had any evil desires living within Him. Sure, the devil presented Him with several offers. Even though these offers were made, it didn't mean that Jesus was tempted to accept any of the proposals. The desire to give in to these offers never entered His heart. Scripture clearly states that a person has experienced temptation when they have already been dragged away by their evil desires. Temptation is not the act of being offered something that you shouldn't have. Temptation is the act of entertaining the possibility of accepting the offer.

Let's say, for example, that you are married. You are at work, and someone of the opposite gender asks you out on a date. The person receiving the offer has not done anything wrong unless he or she entertains the possibility of accepting it. It is when you consider the offer as a possibility that it becomes temptation.

Jesus was never tempted to accept any of the offers Satan made. He didn't have any desire to accept them. Therefore, we can see that James 1:13-18 is correct when it says God cannot be tempted.

It goes on to state in James 1:13-18,

"Then, after desire has conceived, it gives birth to sin; and sin, when it is full-grown, gives birth to death."

This scripture tells us that it might be too late to stop temptation from becoming sin once it has entered our hearts. This verse also describes how sin can ultimately lead to death. This is why it is so essential that we control our desires. Desires come from the heart, and if we have evil desires living within our hearts, we will most likely be led to fulfill those sinful desires. This is why Jesus emphasized so many times that it is not what is on the surface that matters; it's what's within you that matters. (Luke 11:39-41) The heart of a person is the source of all that a person is, whether good or bad. (Proverbs 4:23) This is why we need to fight the problem at its source. We need to train our hearts to desire good things. We need to prepare the heart to resist the temptations of Satan. If we strengthen our hearts, we can become equipped to endure all of this life's challenges.

Luke 22:40

On reaching the place, he said to them, "Pray that you will not fall into temptation."

This scripture reminds us that prayer is one of the best tools we have to defend ourselves against temptation. We know that when we pray for strength to resist temptation, God will hear us. We can be confident of this because, in the book of 1st John 5:14, it states that God will listen to our prayers as long as what we pray for is a part of His will for our lives. We know it is not His will for us to be tempted. After all, temptation does not come from God (James 1:13-18); it comes from the devil.

1 Corinthians 10:13

No temptation has overtaken you, except what is common to mankind. And God is faithful; he will not let you be tempted beyond what you can bear. But when you are tempted, he will also provide a way out so that you can endure it.

The book of 1st Corinthians reminds us that we are not alone in the struggles we face. It tells us that all of humanity is subject to the temptations of this world. As we discussed earlier, Jesus even faced this tactic of the enemy.

This scripture reminds us that God is faithful and will not allow temptation to overcome us. We have the power to resist all temptation through the strength that God gives us. We have to refuse to accept the offers that Satan presents to us.

I believe that we must build up our spiritual strength in order to be able to resist the enemy. We can do this through the study of His Word and prayer. If we have a strong foundation in God and His Word, we can overcome any temptation. (Luke 6:47-49)

Chapter Six

Tactics of the Enemy: Fear

Satan employs many tactics in his attempt to capture our souls. We've already discussed two of those tactics, deception and temptation. The one we are going to discuss in this chapter is fear.

As we dive into the topic of fear, I must begin with this first question: Where does fear come from? If we take a look at this next scripture, we can see that fear does not come from God.

2 Timothy 1:7
God gave us a spirit not of fear, but of power and love and self-control.

In the book of 2 Timothy, we see that God has given us a spirit of love and self-control. God is not the one who has given us a spirit of fear.

Fear is one of the ways that Satan controls us. He uses this strategy because he knows that if he can fill our lives with fear that there will not be room in our hearts for faith. He knows that faith and fear are complete opposites and cannot both exist simultaneously.

When we allow fear to take over our hearts and minds, we allow Satan to manipulate us into distrusting God. Think about it. If we are afraid of a particular circumstance in our life, are we trusting God to handle that circumstance? Is it possible to say to God, "I know you got this," and then continue to be fearful? No, of course not. We can't trust God and then proceed to live in fear. When we live in fear, we live under the enemy's control, not under God's blessing. God offers us the gift of faith. The enemy offers us fear. We are the ones who must choose which one we will accept.

God wants us to trust Him. Here is a scripture that illustrates His desire to give us peace by having us trust in Him.

Deuteronomy 31:8
The Lord himself goes before you and will be with you; he will never leave you nor forsake you. Do not be afraid; do not be discouraged."

In this scripture, we are specifically instructed not to be afraid or discouraged. Why? Because God promises to walk with us through life. Not only does He walk with us - He walks in front of us. He shields us and protects us from the enemy. With God on our side, do we really need to be afraid?

Fear comes into our souls when we forget that God is with us. We must remember that just because God is always with us doesn't mean He will stop fear from entering our lives. We need to acknowledge His presence in our lives. We need to use His presence as a shield. We need to live in His word in order to be able to fight off fear. The Bible says that if we resist the enemy, he will flee. It reminds us that we must take action to overcome fear.

I remember I had gone into a clinic many years ago to get a tetanus shot because I stepped on a rusty old nail while doing some work outside. The nail punctured my skin and caused bleeding to occur. I knew I was long overdue for the vaccination, so I had to get one. When I got to the clinic, the nurse saw that I was nervous. It wasn't that I was afraid of needles; it was the drug inside the needle that scared me. I had a bad experience with a prescription antibiotic a couple of years before this. As a result, I ended up being scared to death of medicine. As I sat there asking dozens of questions while I was trying to delay the inevitable, she stopped for a moment to try to calm my fear by telling me what fear really was. She said to me that fear is nothing more than False Evidence Appearing Real. When I heard this, I realized that it made a lot of sense.

After hearing this explanation of what fear is, I realized that my fear was just an attack from the enemy. He wanted to make sure I didn't do the right thing by seeking the medical treatment that I needed. He used a past experience to act as evidence to support his lies. He tried tirelessly to fill me with so much fear that I would turn right around and walk out of that clinic. Fortunately for me, his attempt failed. God spoke to me through this nurse to help build my faith.

1 John 4:18
Perfect Love Casts Out All Fear

In the book of 1st John, it states that Perfect love casts out all fear. Where can we find perfect love? Can we find it in the relationship we have with our spouse? Can we find it with our children? How about our friends? We love our friends, don't we? Is that where we can find perfect love?

I'm sure many of us have tried looking for perfect love in the arms of another person, only to be disappointed when we found out it wasn't there. Then some of us move on to another, trying to find it somewhere else. No matter how long we search and how far our search takes us, we will never find perfect love if we keep looking in the wrong places.

There is only one place we need to look in our search for perfect love. We need to look up.

God is the only one that can offer us a love so perfect that it can cast out all fear. No one else can do this for us. His love is enough to overcome the enemy.

Since He is love, it makes sense that He can cast out all fear. Why then would we ever look to anyone or anything other than Him?

Psalm 27:1

The lord is my light and my salvation, whom shall I fear? The LORD is the stronghold of my life-- of whom shall I be afraid?

This one says it all. This scripture tells us that as long as we remain focused on God, there is nothing to fear.

As long as we allow God to be our light and salvation, no one can stand against us. When you face difficulties, remember that God is the stronghold of your life. He is your foundation.

When times get tough, the devil will try to fill your soul with fear. When he does this, look to God to be your strength.

Let's take a look at this scripture:

Matthew 10:29-31

Are not two sparrows sold for a penny? Yet not one of them will fall to the ground outside your Father's care. And even the very hairs of your head are all numbered. So, don't be afraid; you are worth more than many sparrows.

What Jesus was saying here was that although sparrows are not considered valuable to people, they are indeed precious to God. In fact, they are so valuable that not one of them could drop from the sky outside of God's will. What I believe this tells us is that there is nothing that can happen to us that is outside of His will. No matter what circumstance we may be facing, I believe that God has equipped us to overcome it.

The truth that we need to understand about fear is that it has no place in a believer's life. So, when fear attacks and tries to raise its head, we must stand firm against it. Remember that He who is in you is greater than he who is in the world. You are the righteousness of God in Christ Jesus.

Stop worrying about what it is you are fearful of. Look to Jesus, who has saved you. Satan has been defeated and has no power over you. Walk in the victory He gave us all at Calvary.

If you do this, you will experience God's peace, which is far more wonderful than the human mind can understand. His peace will guard your hearts and minds as you live in Christ, Jesus. When you have His peace, you cannot be fearful.

When fear comes over you, remember what the nurse said earlier in this chapter: Fear is False Evidence Appearing Real. It is from your old mind or the enemy. Rebuke it.

You have the authority of Jesus, so use it. Command the spirit of fear to leave in the name of Jesus, and it must go. Thank God for giving you peace in the situation. Keep doing it until you feel a release from fear and an infusion of His peace.

Psalm 91:10 NKJV

No evil shall befall you, nor shall any plague come near your dwelling

Don't let the enemy steal your joy and send you off in a direction other than the one the Holy Spirit has for you to take. Hold onto the truth that Jesus is who He says He is and that the enemy cannot overtake you and that no harm shall come to you.

Psalm 23:4

Even though I walk through the darkest valley, I will fear no evil, for you are with me; your rod and your staff, they comfort me.

Psalm 23:4 reminds us that God is always with us to protect us and to comfort us. There is no fear when we remain in Christ.

Focus on who you are in Christ and not the fear we feel in the current circumstances. Fear is a liar.

God knows we tend to be fearful, so He packed the Bible full of reminders that fear has no place in our lives. God gave us the Bible for a reason, and we need to let God use it to breathe peace and life into us through His Holy Spirit. He promises never to leave us nor forsake us. Let's trust Him in this.

Chapter Seven

What if?

Fear doesn't walk alone. Fear usually brings its friends along with it everywhere it goes. Its friends are worry and anxiety. There are many ways the devil can use these three amigos to terrorize us and capture our souls.

How does he do this? One way is through the power of our thoughts. He infiltrates our minds and takes control, no different than someone who hacks into your computer.

The hacker gets in and leaves a virus on your computer's hard drive. If not detected, the virus can wreak havoc on your computer. The computer's processing speed may slow down. It can take longer to open programs and files. The virus can even corrupt files on your computer's hard drive, making it impossible for you to open your Word documents or any of your other programs. Once your computer has been compromised, the hacker can demand payment to unlock your files. The hacker can also erase your entire computer, causing you to lose all of your valuable data. Months of work can be lost in an instant.

The expensive tax preparation software you purchased can be lost, along with all of your family's tax returns that you spent hours preparing. All of that sensitive data can be taken by the hacker. Data such as names, birthdays, and social security numbers can all be compromised.

It's no different than when the lies of the enemy infiltrate our minds. If Satan gains access to something as valuable as our mind, he can control the sensitive data stored there. If this virus is not detected and treated, it can cause utter destruction.

What would you do to protect your computer's critical information? You would most likely install an anti-virus program, or maybe even a firewall. Just like most people would defend their computers with firewalls, we should also protect our minds from the enemy's attacks. We shouldn't let him hack into our hard drives and corrupt us. We have a firewall program we can use to keep unwanted attackers out. It's called the Word of God. Before we begin to discuss how we use the Word of God to defend against Satan's attacks, I want to talk to you about the power of *What if?*

What if is a thought process that the enemy can use to hijack our minds, allowing him to take over and influence our thoughts. Once he successfully injects this poison into our minds, we can become filled with things like worry, fear, and anxiety.

What if can sometimes drive us to always believe in the worst-case scenario. Using the *What if* concept to assume the worst and to anticipate defeat is one of the primary ways in which the devil overtakes us. He tricks us into buying into his *What if* concept. By doing so, we are ultimately giving him the authority that only we, or God can give him. This allows him to entangle our lives in pain, suffering, and defeat.

Have you ever thought, what if my spouse leaves me? Or, what if my child continues to go down the wrong path. What if I lose my job, or my boss cuts my hours?

While I know these things happen all the time, I also know that worrying about them can be detrimental to our well-being. We can't control what may or may not occur in the future. Worrying about *what ifs* will only cause us to be filled with fear and anxiety.

For example, when you're sick, you might be tempted to think, what if I don't get better? Or, what if it gets worse? Satan always wants us to think of the worst-case scenarios. He wants to keep us focused on our pain and suffering. He does this because he knows we have a God who is greater than our worries and fears. God is greater than any circumstance that we could ever find ourselves in. By keeping us focused on all the worst-case scenarios, he can distract us and cause us to lose focus on God.

Think about it like this. You're driving south along the coast of California, admiring the beautiful scenic view. The mighty ocean waves are rushing against the sand. You are breathing in the warm ocean air when you suddenly begin to feel the vibration of your phone. It's alerting you to an incoming text message. What do you do? Just like so many of us would do, you grab the phone out of your pocket and begin reading the message. Rather than enjoying the breathtaking view of nature, you allow yourself to become distracted. We do this because we don't realize that all it takes is just one small distraction to cause us to lose control of the car and swerve off the road over the cliff, plunging hundreds of feet downward towards our destruction.

This is what happens when we allow the devil to distract us with all the *what-ifs* that he is continually trying to whisper into our ears. He is the one that is texting us all of these negative *what if* thoughts, causing us to lose control and crash. We need to ignore these *what if* messages and remain focused on the road. The beautiful scenery (God's creation) is all around us. We should enjoy all that God has to offer us, rather than be distracted by the lies of the enemy. God offers us hope, peace, and eternal salvation. It's no wonder why Satan is trying to distract us. He doesn't want us to have these blessings.

Let's talk about one of my *what ifs*. I run a tax preparation business. My income is determined by how many customers walk through the doors. I have very little control over this. I can hire and train my employees and do all the marketing in the world, but ultimately, I can't force people to choose our company over the competition. There are so many unknown variables. When you own a business, you lack the security of having a guaranteed paycheck. With the lack of security and the financial risks involved in owning your own business, it can be very easy to worry about the future. Throughout the years, I have found myself thinking, what if we have a decrease in sales this tax season? If this happens, I won't be able to pay my bills. Then, after-tax season ends, I look at my bank account, and wonder, what if this isn't enough money to get us through the end of the year?

I don't understand why I have these *what if* worries. I've been a business owner for almost 20 years now, and I can tell you that I have never gone without everything I need. I never said I didn't struggle throughout the years. There were years where I was deep in debt. When I say deep in debt, I'm talking about hundreds of thousands of dollars in debt.

I can tell you that I struggled financially throughout the years, but no matter what, I always had a roof over my head and food on the table. There were times in the past when the only food I could afford to put on the table was Ramen noodles. Due to God's blessings, there have also been times where I have been able to enjoy a filet mignon lifestyle as well.

My point is that my *what if* worries have always been based upon my fear of the worst-case scenario happening. Now, this is no way for a person to live their life. There is no need for all of this worry, fear, and anxiety. Why would a person choose to live like this?

Luke 12:25 says, "Who of you by worrying can add a single hour to your life." Worrying about negative *what ifs* doesn't add anything to our lives. It takes away from our lives. The time we spend worrying

about the *what-ifs* is wasted. The peace we can ha[ve in]
life is lost while we worry about these *what ifs*. [W]
about joy? Can we have joy while the weight of worry
is on our shoulders?

I know for me, another area of my life that causes
me to focus on the *what ifs* is my health. Throughout
the years of my life, I have faced medical challenges
that have left doctors confused. I've been diagnosed
with things like diabetes, herniated discs in my neck
and back, arthritis in my knees, tendonitis in my
elbows, tinnitus in one of my ears, heart dysfunction, a
kidney cyst, liver damage, and worst of all, brain
damage. So, needless to say, each time I'm diagnosed
with something new, the wheels in my head begin to
spin, and all the *what ifs* start to race through my mind.

You can imagine the web of *what ifs* that can arise
from all of these things. You can also imagine how
difficult it could be to maneuver your way through this
web, trying not to get entangled in it, leaving yourself
vulnerable to be consumed by the black widow herself.
Now, if you're not careful, this is precisely what will
happen to you. I found myself wandering through this
maze, only to realize that I was on the path towards
worry, fear, and anxiety.

Thankfully, I would never remain on this path for
long. I would always come back. How would I do
this, you ask? It's simple. I follow the light. You see,
there is always a light shining in our lives. This light
can show us the way. This light that I speak of is Jesus.
This is a light that no force of darkness could ever

stand against. I believe that once you begin to follow this light, you will realize that you can never get lost.

Over the years of my life, the devil has filled my mind with tons of *What if* thoughts. He's injected these negative thoughts into my mind so much that I actually talked about it in my last book, **The Promise.** I wrote an entire chapter about it. I think it was the longest chapter in the whole book. Here is an excerpt from my last book:

I also heard a lot of evil what ifs in my heart. What if the doctor accidentally tears an artery while navigating the instrument through my arteries, and I bleed out on the table? What if the anesthesiologist gives me too much anesthesia and I never wake up?

After several days of this, I realized this is the devil, and all the evil "What ifs" are coming from him. Instead, I decided to think only about good, godly things.

What if the procedure ends up going well? What if the doctor finds nothing wrong and I'm free to move forward with my wedding? What if....?

In these paragraphs above, I talked about a medical procedure that I was scheduled to have done several years ago. At the time, I was only 39 years old, and my doctor told me that my heart was severely dysfunctional.

Can you imagine how easy it was for the devil to take control of my thoughts and fill my mind with negative *What ifs*? As I described in the last paragraph of the excerpt, I had to focus on God and His power, rather than focusing on the enemy's tactics.

Here's another excerpt from my last book:

Of course, I would wonder, what if I was wrong? What if I misunderstood what I believed God had told me? What if it wasn't God. What if it was the devil who had told me this, with a plan of deceiving me into a trap that would ultimately consume us all. Our lives were literally at stake, with the realistic possibility that she might hurt him greater than she ever had before and that she would once again attempt to take my life, possibly being successful this time around. My freedom and my everything was at stake. I gambled it all on a promise that God had made twelve and a half years earlier

In this excerpt, I talked about how God promised me He would bring my son home from his biological mother. My son's mother had a mental illness and was extremely violent and abusive. My son and I were facing the greatest battle of our lives. We were in the middle of custody litigation that had erupted like a volcano. Ash and burning hot lava were spewing out everywhere, consuming everything in its path.

During this challenging time in our lives, Satan tried to question God's integrity. He wanted to make me doubt God's word. I could hear him whisper in my ear, "What if God doesn't keep His promise?" He tried to fill me with so much worry and fear that I couldn't help but think, what if I'm destined to lose this battle? The enemy had me thinking that I should give up and surrender. Giving up is precisely what he wanted me to do. That's why he was trying to fill my head with doubt and fear.

It didn't work, though. When you continue to read further into my last book, you will see that the devil's attempt to steal my faith had failed.

The devil's *what ifs* still enter into my mind at times, but nowadays, they are merely passing through. Sometimes it takes effort to push out those negative thoughts. Sometimes it takes prayer. Sometimes it just takes time reading God's word.

Let's turn the page in our discussion of the *what if* thought process and look at how we can use it to our advantage. Let's take a look at this next excerpt from my last book, **The Promise**:

I never thought, "What if" my son ends up living with me full time, seven days a week, 365 days a year. Never did I think, "What if" this ends in the termination of her parental rights, and we move on to live happily ever after. I never thought, "What if" God brings my baby home and allows my new wife that He blessed me with to adopt my son, giving him the positive female role model that he had always lacked. Never did I think of these "What ifs."

In this paragraph taken from my last book, I find myself admitting that during some of the toughest times in my life, I never stopped to think of the *What if* concept from God's perspective. When I looked through the lenses of darkness, all I could see was the negative *what if*s. What if I lose this battle? *What if, What if, What if?* While I believed in God's promise to move the heavens and the earth to make a way for my son, I never really thought that His promise meant anything more than me going from having 43% custody of my son to just 51 %. I would have considered that the victory He had promised. At the time, I had never thought of the greater *what ifs* that I would end up writing about.

As I look back, I realize I could've lived my life back then with a lot more peace, faith, hope, and a lot less worry, fear, and anxiety, had I just recognized the authority that God gives us.

There are many scriptures that describe how God has given us authority over the enemy. Had I remained focused on God and not distracted by the negative *what ifs*, I could have used my thoughts to focus on the positive *what ifs*, strengthening my faith.

Take the *what ifs* and use them for your good. Use them to build your faith. Rather than all the negative *what ifs* that you hear, start proclaiming the positive *what ifs*. Like, what if God heals me? What if I get a promotion at work? What if everything does work out in my favor? *What if?*

Don't let the enemy lie to you, telling you that things are never going to get better. Don't let him *deceive* you into thinking that there is no hope. Do not allow him to *tempt* you into believing that God is not in control. And never allow the enemy to fill you with so much *fear* that all you hear are negative *what ifs*.

Do what I do when the devil uses his tactics of *deception, temptation,* and *fear* to fill my mind with negative *what ifs*. Take the Word of God and use it as a weapon. Just like Jesus did when Satan tried to tempt Him, quote scripture to him. Let him know who's in charge.

While I recognize that prayer is a powerful tool in our spiritual lives, I also believe that in addition to talking to God about our problems, we also need to speak to our problems and tell them how powerful our God is. When the enemy attacks, tell him that our God is greater than he is. When the devil whispers in your ears, *what if_____*, scream back at him, *what if my God_____*.

The devil knows he can't defeat you without you first permitting him to do so. Remind him of *his* weaknesses. Remind him of *his* limits. Remind him that he is *not* in control.

When you face these negative *what ifs* from the enemy, remember to look at the circumstances through God's eyes. When we look through the eyes of God, we will be able to see things as God sees them. We will be able to see hope that has no limits. We will be able to see a future that is greater than anything in our past. We will be able to see the mercy, grace, and peace of a God that will love us forever.

Chapter Eight

Faith

We've talked a lot about the enemy's greatest weapons, such as deception, temptation, and fear. It's now time to talk about one of our greatest weapons, and that is faith.

Faith can be a powerful thing. The Bible mentions it hundreds of times. The Bible presents many examples of the power that faith has. Before we talk about the power that it has, let us first examine what the Bible says that faith is.

Hebrews 11:1

Now faith is the substance of things hoped for, the evidence of things not seen.

One of our world's best-known scientists, Carl Sagan, was once quoted as saying, "Faith is believing in something in the absence of evidence."

I can understand how a person could believe such a thing, but I must strongly disagree with his opinion. According to the Bible, faith is the opposite of what this talented scientist thought it to be. Hebrews 11:1 describes faith as something tangible. It describes faith as the *evidence* of things not seen and that faith is the *substance* of things hoped for.

The Bible teaches us that faith is more than just hope. It shows us that it is an assurance. Let's look at these scriptures below to see how faith has manifested itself into something more than just hope.

Mark 10:52
And Jesus said to him, "Go, for your faith has healed you." Instantly the man could see, and he followed Jesus down the road.

Mark 5:34
And he said to her, "Daughter, your faith has made you well. Go in peace. Your suffering is over."

Matthew 9:27-31
As Jesus went on from there, two blind men followed him, calling out, "Have mercy on us, Son of David!" When he had gone indoors, the blind men came to him, and he asked them, "Do you believe that I am able to do this?" "Yes, Lord," they replied. Then he touched their eyes and said, "According to your faith let it be done to you"; and their sight was restored. Jesus warned them sternly, "See that no one knows about this." But they went out and spread the news about him all over that region.

These scriptures account for several occasions where people were healed of their illnesses and disabilities due to their faith. They also illustrate the power that faith has in the hands of a believer. These scriptures teach us that faith can manifest into the tangible fulfillment of the things that the person with the faith is hoping for.

How about you? Do you have faith that God will answer your prayers? Has your faith been so great that God used it to give you what it is you were praying for?

I've had faith that manifested into the fulfillment of what my faith had hoped for. In my last book, **The Promise,** I told the story of how God promised me He would save my son from his abusive mother and bring him home to me. For more than a decade, I had to watch as my son lived a life filled with abuse and fear. There was no *evidence* that God's promise was going to be fulfilled. My eyes couldn't see a way for this to happen. Everyone in the world told me it was impossible and that it couldn't be done. The absence of evidence didn't stop me from holding on to my faith in God's promise. My faith survived through all the trials and tribulations, through all the disappointments, and all of the pain. My faith survived because I placed my faith in the One who always provides for us, the One who gives us the strength to survive, and the One who is greater than all the adversities that come against us.

It is because of the fulfillment of God's promise in my life that I can testify to the truth of Hebrews 11:1. I can prove that faith is not merely believing in something in the absence of evidence. I can testify that faith *is* the evidence of things not seen and that it *is* the substance of things hoped for.

Now that we have discussed what faith is, let's talk about where faith comes from.

Romans 10:17

So, faith comes from hearing; that is, hearing the Good News about Christ.

In the book of Romans, God's word tells us that faith comes from hearing the good news about Jesus Christ. This is the only way I could imagine that faith is born. The good news about Jesus Christ is by far the most significant source of strength I have ever been able to find. I am so overwhelmed when I think about His love for us and the sacrifice He made for us. Knowing He healed the sick and brought the dead back to life assures me that my faith is justified. I can be confident in my faith because Jesus is the foundation for my faith. And in Him, and through Him, I know that my faith will allow the will of God to manifest in my life.

Romans 12:3

For by the grace given to me I say to everyone among you not to think of himself more highly than he ought to think, but to think with sober judgment, each according to the measure of faith that God has assigned.

This scripture tells us that God has assigned each of us a measure of faith. What does this mean? First, it means that faith is a gift from God. It is not something we earned. It is given to us out of His heart of generosity.

After reading this scripture, I can certainly understand how it could raise a couple of questions. The first question a person could ask is this: If God gives each of us a measure of faith, why is it that some people don't have any?

Well, let me tell you what I believe. I believe that just like any other gift that is offered to us, in order to receive it, we must first accept it.

Think of it like this. It's Christmas time, and you have a friend that mails you a present every year. If the present is valuable enough, the sender might require you to provide a signature to make sure you receive the gift. The mail carrier will walk up to your door, knock, and when you open the door, he or she will attempt to collect a signature from you and then deliver the package. At that moment, you must choose whether you want to accept it or not. If you decide to sign for the package, you will receive it. If you decide not to sign for the package, the carrier will take it back, and stamp *Return to Sender* on it, and it will go back to the person that mailed it.

The gifts God offers us are the same. To receive the gift, we must accept it. God will not force us to take it. We are created with a free will and can choose to refuse any gift he offers us. This is the reason why some people have faith and others don't.

The next question someone might ask is: If God assigns us a measure of faith, meaning that He gives us a predetermined amount, how could I grow my faith?

Then you might be led to wonder, what if He hasn't given me enough? What if the amount of faith He has given me is less than the amount He gave someone else? How would that fair? If God gives us each a measure of faith, how do I make sure I get my fair share? It's simple. I believe God gives us more faith than we could ever need. I believe He provides us with a measure of faith so considerable that it could last us one hundred lifetimes. The faith He gives us is enough to allow us to do the things that Jesus told us we could do with it. All we need to do is learn how to harness the power of our faith and use it to allow God's will to manifest in our lives. I truly believe that He has given us an unlimited measure of faith.

For example, think back to when you were a kid, and your parents took you to the county fair when it came to town. Do you remember the fun you had going on the rides, eating cotton candy, and playing all of those games with the hope of winning a prize?

Do you remember the test of strength game? This game allowed you to test your strength by hitting a lever with a sledgehammer. If you were able to hit the lever hard enough, you could watch the puck rise to the top, then hit the bell, and you would win a prize.

That's kind of how faith works. The measure of faith God gives us is so high that we have access to more than we could ever imagine. What determines how much faith we can reach or acquire is based upon how strong we are or how hard we hit the lever.

How does a person acquire enough physical strength to hit the bell at the top and reach their maximum potential? By exercising and strengthening their muscles.

Faith is no different. To reach the full measure of faith God has assigned to us, we must exercise our faith. We can build our faith by hearing the Word of God. We can strengthen our faith through prayer, reading the Bible, and fellowship with other believers.

If you are experiencing difficulties in your life and feel as though your faith isn't strong enough to carry you through, you can rest assured that God has assigned you more than enough faith. All you need to do is build your faith through the methods we just discussed.

Faith is indeed a gift from God. And because He is a limitless God, the amount of faith that He offers us is also limitless.

We just discussed what faith is and where it comes from. The question now is, do we understand how powerful it is?

Matthew 17:10
Truly I tell you, if you have faith as small as a mustard seed, you can say to this mountain, 'Move

from here to there,' and it will move. Nothing will be impossible for you."

In this scripture, Jesus was quoted as saying that with faith as small as a mustard seed, we can tell mountains to move, and they would move. I think we can all agree that Jesus was speaking metaphorically. The mountains He was talking about are the problems and difficulties that we all face. He was saying that we can overcome all of life's adversities with just a small amount of faith. Understand that it is not in our strength alone that we can overcome all of life's troubles. It is in His strength that we can overcome all of life's mountains.

The power of faith is well documented throughout the Bible. We discussed several scriptures earlier in this chapter that tells us how faith can heal. Faith is limitless in its ability to accomplish God's will in our life.

Let's look at one more scripture that shows us what faith can do.

Luke 5:17-26

On one of the days, while Jesus was teaching, some proud religious law-keepers and teachers of the Law were sitting by Him. They had come from every town in the countries of Galilee and Judea and from Jerusalem. The power of the Lord was there to heal them. Some men took a man who was not able to move his body to Jesus. He was carried on a bed. They looked for a way to take the man into the house where Jesus was. But they could not find a way to take him in because of so many people. They made a hole in the roof over where Jesus stood. Then they let the bed with the sick man on it down before Jesus. When Jesus saw their faith, He said to the man, "Friend, your sins are forgiven."

The teachers of the Law and the proud religious law-keepers thought to themselves, "Who is this Man Who speaks as if He is God? Who can forgive sins but God only?" Jesus knew what they were thinking. He said to them, "Why do you think this way in your hearts? Which is easier to say, 'Your sins are forgiven,' or, 'Get up and walk'?

"So that you may know the Son of Man has the right and the power on earth to forgive sins," He said to the man who could not move his body, "I say to you, get up. Take your bed and go to your home." At once, the sick man got up in front of them. He took his bed and went to his home, thanking God. All those who were there were surprised and gave thanks to God, saying, "We have seen very special things today."

In this scripture, we see how Jesus recognized the faith of the disabled man's friends. These men knew that if they could bring their friend to Jesus, that Jesus would heal him. They had to believe this because if they didn't, they would not have gone through all the trouble of climbing onto the roof and lowering him down to Jesus. They could have walked up to the house where Jesus was, and seen the crowd and thought to themselves, "Never mind, there are too many people here. We will never be able to get to Jesus. It's impossible." Instead of giving up, they decided not to allow the absence of a path to stop them from reaching their destination. In other words, they made a way where there seemed to be no way.

Isn't that what God does? Doesn't He make a way where there appears to be no way? God has done it for me. He has moved mountains in my life.

In April 2013, my dad's cardiologist told us that he only expected my dad to live another six months. This was after having several open-heart surgeries, more than a half a dozen stents surgically placed into his arteries, and two pacemakers placed in his chest. It has been more than six years since we were told this, and my dad is still alive and doing well. All of these variables were not enough to stop God from making a way where there was no way.

After several attorneys told me for many years that there was no way I would be able to get full custody of my son because of the gender discrimination in family courts, God finally brought him home to me in 2017, just like He promised He would. In the natural, there was no way. That didn't stop God from making a way.

The Gospel of Luke tells us how these men made a path to Jesus. They couldn't get through the crowd, so they went around the crowd. They didn't stand there feeling sorry for themselves. They had the faith that was needed to move the mountain that was standing in their way. They didn't give up. They went up. They climbed the mountain and made it to the top.

When they did this, they showed Jesus the strength of their faith. What happened when Jesus saw their strength? He moved the disabled man's mountain. That mountain was a life of sin that had left the man's soul without life. When Jesus forgave him of his sins, his soul was reborn. The power of the spirit that was now living within him allowed his body to rise again. Not only did he rise and walk, but he also carried his belongings with him as he walked home.

No longer did he need to be carried, and no longer was he unable to move. Instead, he was moved by the Holy Spirit of God. This is what faith had done for him. The faith of this man's friends caused Jesus to move the mountains surrounding this man's life, body, and soul.

This is a powerful example of what faith can do. There are many more scriptures that describe the power of faith. These were just a couple of examples of its power and its purpose.

Chapter Nine

The Power of Our Thoughts

While doing some research for this chapter of my book, I ran into this quote made by a man named Frank Jackson. This is what he said.

Watch your thoughts, for they become words. Watch your words, for they become actions. Watch your actions, for they become habits. Watch your habits, for they become character. Watch your character for it will become your destiny.

There is a lot of truth in this quote. It illustrates the connection between each of these things, and it reminds us that our thoughts lead to our actions. If we have good thoughts, it will lead to good actions. If we have evil thoughts, it will lead to evil acts. It also connects our actions to the formation of habits, which we know can be hard to break. A lifetime of habits, good or bad, end up defining our characters and ultimately our destinies.

Because our destinies are ultimately formed from our thoughts, it is crucial that we learn how to control our thoughts so they don't take us captive. We need to hold our thoughts captive and use them to create the destiny that we desire.

Numerous scriptures tell us about the power of our thoughts, how to control them, and what happens when we don't.

The first scripture I want to discuss is in the book of Proverbs.

Proverbs 4:23
Above all else, guard your heart, for everything you do flows from it.

I love the book of Proverbs. It is one of my favorite books in the Bible. It contains a lot of wisdom and great advice. This particular verse is no exception.

This scripture warns us to guard what is possibly the most valuable asset that we possess. This verse tells us that the heart is where it all begins. Everything we do comes from it.

The Bible also tells us in Jeremiah 17:19 that *the heart is deceitful above all things. Who can understand it?* This means that the enemy has access to our hearts through his tactics of deception, fear, and temptation. He can use these weapons to infect our hearts with a virus that can take over our lives. We must be careful not to allow this to happen. This is why we are told to guard our hearts.

If we let the wrong things in, it can contaminate us at our very core. This is why it is important to be careful about what we watch on tv, what music we listen to, and what friends we choose to surround ourselves with. It's easy to see the connection between what we take in and what we put out.

Have you ever heard of the saying; *you are what you eat*? That saying holds a lot of truth. If you don't eat well, your health will suffer; if you eat well, your body should remain healthy.

Do you think professional football players and Olympic athletes put a lot of junk food into their bodies? I don't think so. They know they must take care of their body in order to increase their ability to perform. Part of their training plan typically includes proper nutrition, rest, and physical training.

When it comes to our spiritual performance, it's no different. We must be careful about what we allow into our hearts and even who we allow in our hearts.

This next scripture describes in more detail how a corrupt heart can cause us to sin against God.

Mark 7:20-23

He went on: "What comes out of a person is what defiles them. For it is from within, out of a person's heart, those evil thoughts come—sexual immorality, theft, murder, adultery, greed, malice, deceit, lewdness, envy, slander, arrogance, and folly. All these evils come from inside and defile a person."

The Bible tells us that evil thoughts come from the heart. We know that our thoughts can sometimes give birth to actions. If we are not careful, those actions can sometimes get us into trouble.

A lot of the horrific things that people do in this world often begin as a thought. What we need to do is choose to overcome the evil thoughts that manifest inside of us. We need to keep our hearts pure so the thoughts that flow from it cause us to live a victorious life.

Let's look at this next scripture.

Philippians 4:8
Whatever is noble, whatever is right, whatever is pure, whatever is lovely, whatever is admirable—if anything is excellent or praiseworthy—think about such things.

This scripture tells us to focus our thoughts on good things. By doing so, we can train ourselves to be strong enough to resist the enemy's attacks.

Remember, it's just like looking through a microscope. The things we focus on get magnified. This is why we must focus on *whatever is noble, whatever is right, whatever is pure, whatever is lovely,* and *whatever is admirable*

This is why I start my day by thanking God for all He is and all He has done in my life. I roll out of bed praising Him each morning. I thank Him for the great day He is about to bless me with.

After doing this, I walk downstairs to begin the rest of my day with breakfast and a cup of coffee. But before I hit the button on the Keurig, I start playing a podcast on my phone. I go into the podcast app and see Joel Osteen and Joyce Meyer staring back at me from my telephone screen. I usually spend a moment browsing through the sermon titles, trying to get a feel for what message I need on that particular day. After a few moments, one of them will catch my attention. I click the play button and begin my morning dose of God's word. It's only after the Word of God begins to flow through my soul that I have the strength to press the button on the Keurig.

I move on to the upstairs bathroom after breakfast, where I begin cleaning myself up for the day ahead of me. I continue feeding my soul with the Word of God as I listen to one of my favorite preachers speak to me through the tiny speaker on my phone.

After I'm done getting ready for work, I sometimes rest outside on my front porch while I admire the beauty of God's creation. I like to watch the trees as the wind gently pushes against their leaves. I listen to the sound of the birds chirping as I open a book from one of my favorite authors. I turn the pages until I find where I left off and continue reading.

I love to read Joel Osteen and Joyce Myers books. I also like inspirational biographies, like, *I Still Believe*, from Christian musician Jeremy Camp. I enjoy learning about the path that others have taken towards God and His will for their lives. It is encouraging to hear their stories of how God has carried them through all of their trials and tribulations.

These are the things I do each morning to equip myself for whatever the enemy might try to bring against me. I have been around long enough to know that the devil doesn't rest. He doesn't take a day off, and neither should you or I. We must be prepared at all times by equipping ourselves with the weapons that God has given us to fight off the enemy. The Bible tells us what we should do in order to live the blessed life that God has given us.

The Bible continues to tell us how we can use our thoughts to guide us towards God. Let's look at this next scripture.

Romans 12:2

Do not conform to the pattern of this world, but be transformed by the renewing of your mind. Then you will be able to test and approve what God's will is— his good, pleasing and perfect will.

This scripture tells us we must be transformed by the renewing of our minds. How do we do that? By following the instructions in Philippians 4:8. We must focus our thoughts and our minds on the Word of God.

What I find remarkable about this scripture is it tells us that once we are transformed by the renewing our minds, we will be able to test and approve God's will.

I can't help but ask myself, who am I that I should be given the authority to test God? Who am I that He would allow me to approve His will for my life?

This scripture tells us that He has permitted us to choose between His will and our will. We can choose to follow His plan for our lives or choose to go down our own path.

I don't feel as though I deserve to have the freedom to choose my will rather than His. After all, Jesus is the one who paid for my salvation with His blood. I've done nothing to deserve this freedom. He gave His life as a sacrifice for mine.

So how do I decide between His will and mine? The answer to this question is simple. I don't have to choose. Why? Because I have allowed myself to be transformed by the renewing of my mind. I have been changed in a way that has left my heart to desire His will for my life. I do not have to choose one or the other because they are now the same.

My will for my life is identical to His will for my life. There is no longer a choice to make. I have already chosen to die to myself and surrender my life to Him.

When you choose to do this, you are no longer your own person. You become a true child of God. You belong to Him. You were bought and paid for with the sacrifice that Jesus made at Calvary. No longer do you live with your own selfish desires. You and Christ now live as one. This is how the renewing of your mind transforms you.

We must understand that this is a process and that it takes effort. We must choose this for ourselves. It will not happen automatically. Remember that God gave us free will. We must choose to renew our minds every day.

he word *renew* means to make new what was once
Our mind is not the same today as it was
yesterday. Time has passed. Life happens to us every
day. We must learn to renew our minds daily with the
Word of God. Failing to do so will leave us with the
old thoughts that had led us away from God in the past.
Failing to renew our minds with the Word of God will
ultimately allow Satan to penetrate our minds and our
thoughts with the temptations and fear that he has used
before to try to take us away from God.

Let's move on to the next scripture.

Isaiah 55:8

*"For my thoughts are not your thoughts, neither are
your ways my ways," declares the Lord.*

In this scripture, God reminds us that we are not to
compare ourselves to Him. Although we are created in
His image, we still have a free will. Because of this
free will, we are not necessarily going to share the
same thoughts that God has, nor will we have the same
ways as Him.

It is more than our free will that separates us from
God. The fact that we are the creation, and He is the
creator, also separates us. We simply do not know
what He knows. We never will.

We all remember what happened when Eve took a
bite out of the apple from the tree of knowledge of
good and evil, right? Eve wanted to be like God. She
wanted to have His knowledge. Little did Eve know

that she was not equipped to understand the things that God understands. She didn't realize that ignorance really can be blissful. Not knowing everything can sometimes be a good thing. However, the devil tempted and deceived Eve into thinking it was ok to eat the fruit. He does this to us every day. At least he tries to.

We need to understand that while our thoughts are not God's thoughts, we must continually strive to make our thoughts more like His. The only way we can do this is to consume as much of His Word as possible every day. We need to spend time with Him in prayer. We need to get to know Him.

Do you know how married couples can sometimes finish each other's sentences? They can do that because they have spent a lot of time getting to know each other. They know each other well enough to anticipate what the other spouse is going to say. That's what we need to do with God. We need to get to know Him and His will for our lives.

This last scripture we are going to look at in this chapter is in the book of Proverbs.

Proverbs 23:7
As someone thinks within himself, so he is.

What more can I say other than WOW! There is no beating around the bush here with this one. It gets straight to the point.

Have you ever considered this? That you are what you think? This is why so many people suffer from depression. We grow up thinking about the thoughts of this world. The thoughts that have been infused into our minds by the people around us. Thoughts that have been drilled into our hearts since we were born. Everywhere you look, there is someone there telling you what you should think.

Let's take the media, for example. Hundreds of millions of dollars are spent each year by corporations to convince you that you need their product. If you want to look good, you must wear our clothing. If you're going to be respected, then you must drive our cars. These companies aren't merely telling you to buy their products. They spend a fortune trying to convince you that you need their products.

It's one thing to say, "Try this; I bet you will like it." However, the marketing that we are exposed to goes way beyond that. The ads that they throw at us are designed to influence our purchasing decisions by altering our thoughts of what is socially acceptable and what isn't. For an ad to be effective, the advertiser needs to make you think that you have to have their product.

Take telephones, for example. How many of us rush to buy the latest and greatest iPhone that comes out? Why is it that the one you bought 12 months ago isn't good enough anymore? Do you need a new telephone or do you want it? Could you live without it? Of course you could.

Apple wouldn't make any money if they didn't convince you that you needed the latest and greatest technology. I find that the upgrades made to each phone aren't significant enough to justify spending another $1,000 to $1,200 on a new one. It may be a little faster and take better pictures. So what? I'm happy with the phone I've had for the past year. If the new iPhone never existed, I would never care to have it. I would be content with what I have. However, because all my friends are upgrading to the latest and greatest, I would feel bad if I didn't upgrade also. The whole *keeping up with the Jones* mentality makes me think that I have to have this new phone to fit in.

This is how companies like Apple have capitalized on our desire to compete with our neighbors. They know that human nature makes us want to covet thy neighbors' belongings. If they can make it cool to have an iPhone, and always make it cool to have the latest and greatest, then they can persuade us to think that we need to have it too.

On the news the other day, I saw how national fast-food restaurants like Burger King, Wendy's, and McDonald's give away annual passes to celebrities. They hope that if you see your favorite celebrity on the cover of a tabloid eating a burger at their restaurant, it will make their restaurant the place everyone wants to be.

People everywhere are trying to influence our thoughts for one reason or another. Usually, it is for their own personal gain. It's either to sell you something or to make you do what they want you to do.

The world will try to make you think that you have to look a certain way to be liked. Society will tell you that you have to make a lot of money to have value. Fortunately for us, these things are not true.

What the world is doing is making us feel like we are not good enough. When it does this, it takes our hearts and thoughts captive. By doing so, the enemy can control you. The devil can hold you down. He doesn't want you to be aware of the fact that Christ died for our sins, and through Him, we can have new life. If he can keep you thinking that you are worthless and can keep you from realizing your real value, he can keep you from all the blessings that God has planned for your life.

Satan works through all outlets that will allow him to operate. This is even true for you. He will work through you, to take you down, and to take down everyone around you. How does he do this? He attacks your thoughts. He makes you think that you are less than. He makes you believe that you are not enough. If he can accomplish this, he can use you to spread this lie to those around you.

Do not let the devil hold your thoughts hostage. Do not let him direct your mind. Our mind is a powerful thing. It controls our entire body. It is the processor, motherboard, and hard drive all wrapped up in one. It holds our *computer's* operating system. If we allow him to inject a virus onto our operating system, we are doomed to crash.

We can defend ourselves from these attacks by using the word of God to protect ourselves.

Chapter Ten

The Power of our Words

Words are a fantastic thing. They are one of the few things in life that have as much power as they do. The power they yield is comparable to the power of a mighty ruler.

Imagine being ruler over all the earth. Imagine the kind of power you would have. Take a look at the highest position here on earth, which most Americans would consider to be the United States' Presidency. That position is filled with great power. Our President can change the world with just the swipe of a pen. I'm sure he signs many executive orders throughout his time as leader of the free world.

There are many bills that pass-through Congress and make it to his desk for his approval. One signature is all it takes to have such a profound impact on the history of our planet.

In 1776, when our founding fathers inked the most important document in our nation's history, the Declaration of Independence, they did so with the stroke of a pen. What is significant about what they did is that they used words to declare their independence. They wrote a document that established themselves as a sovereign nation.

These were some of the most powerful words ever to be written. They changed the history of the world. These words created a nation that would become one of the most powerful countries on earth.

Think about how powerful those words were. Our founding fathers declared what they desired and wrote those words down on paper. In essence, they did what we are instructed to do in the book of Romans, where it says we are to call things that are not as though they are.

It took an enormous amount of faith to declare something as bold as what they did. Let's face it, just because they declared their independence didn't mean England would recognize it. In fact, England didn't recognize the words written on that piece of paper. That's why we had to fight for our freedom. The revolutionary war lasted for many years, and many lives were lost. All of this happened over words. I know there was a lot more to the story than that, but I think you understand what I mean.

Words have changed the world. Just take a look at the greatest book of all time, the Bible. The words that have been recorded in this book have had a profound impact on billions of lives. The Bible records the inspired Word of God. It is filled with wisdom, truth, and stories that teach us about our creator.

A lot of Jesus' ministry is recorded within the pages of this great book. Some of the miracles He performed while here on earth were written down so that all of humanity can know the love that God has for us.

The four gospels of the new testament share with us the greatest love story in the history of our world. In this incredible true story, we learn that Jesus loved us so much that He sacrificed His life for us so we can be saved from our sins.

These are only a couple of examples of the impact that words have had on our lives and the history of this earth. When we begin to study the Word of God, we can find many references to words and the power they possess.

The book of Genesis tells us how God created the heavens and the earth with His words. He simply spoke it all into existence. The significance of this is that, according to the Bible, we are created in God's image. As a result, our words have similar authority as His.

Have you ever heard the phrase, *Sticks and stones will break my bones, but names (words) will never hurt me*? I remember hearing this when I was a child.

According to Wikipedia, it is an old children's rhyme intended to persuade the child victim of name-calling to ignore the taunt and refrain from physical retaliation.

One of the earliest known publications of this children's rhyme is reported to have taken place sometime in March 1862 in *The Christian Recorder,* a publication of the African Methodist Episcopal Church.

It amazes me to think that all these years ago, people believed that words didn't matter. When I was a child, my parents told me to say these words to anyone who tried to be mean to me. It was intended to let the aggressor understand that you didn't care if they called you a bad name. It was a way to teach kids how to deal with the inevitable childhood experience of being bullied.

While this may have helped maintain the peace on the school playgrounds, it did nothing in terms of teaching one of life's greatest truths. This truth is simple. Words have power.

Let's look at this scripture.

Proverbs 18:21
The tongue has the power of life and death, and those who love it will eat its fruit.

This scripture reminds us that our words do have the power to bring life or death into the world.

Has there ever been a time when someone at work talked about you behind your back? Do you think that the gossip they are spreading is bringing life to you and your character? No, it isn't. It's doing the opposite. When people talk about you behind your back, they are usually saying things that are not very nice. These negative things that are said about you bring death to your character. Whoever is listening to the gossip is being persuaded to believe negative things about you. Whether the things being said are true or not doesn't matter. Those negative words are killing your character in the minds of those that are hearing them. This is an excellent example of how words can have the power of death in our lives.

What I believe is worse than someone else speaking negative words over our life is when we do it ourselves. How often do you catch yourself saying things like, "I can't do this; it's impossible," Or, "Nothing good ever happens to me." When things are stressing you out, you might say something like, "I can't take it anymore. This is going to drive me crazy."

How often do we speak these kinds of negative words over our lives and not even realize it? Do we understand that if we believe the challenge is impossible to overcome, then it will be? If you tell yourself that the stress is going to drive you crazy, then it probably will.

We have power over our circumstances. We have the authority to direct our lives with our words. Yes, there are going to situations in our lives that we may not have control over. And yes, there will be times when we face difficulties that may appear to be more than what we can handle. What we need to do is surrender to God rather than to the circumstances.

Have you ever wanted to apply for a promotion at work, but you don't because you're afraid of being denied? Have you told yourself, "I'm not qualified for the job. I don't have the right education. I don't have enough experience. It will never happen."?

Since when has God required you to be qualified in order to receive His blessings? Was David qualified to receive his promotion? Did he have enough experience to go to battle with Goliath? No, he didn't. The great thing about God's blessings is that you don't have to do anything to qualify for them. He blesses His children out of love.

When we talk about the power of our word's, I can't help but think of a song by Christian musician Toby Mac called *Speak Life*. The lyrics of this song can remind us that we have the power to change the lives of people around us with the words we say. He says in his song; *We can turn a heart through the words we say, Mountains crumble with every syllable, hope can live or die.*

These words are so true. We can bring a smile to someone's face with a simple compliment. We can show our gratitude by saying thank you. We can make someone's day better by sharing a few kind words.

Here's another excellent scripture to think of when we talk about the power of our words:

Proverbs 15:1 *A gentle answer turns away wrath, but a harsh word stirs up anger.*

My son and I were at a restaurant one afternoon a couple of months ago. While we were there, we noticed that our waitress was very rude to us. My son asked me why she was behaving that way. I explained to him that sometimes people go through struggles in their personal life that causes them to be irritable.

I reminded him that I get that way when my back hurts or when work stresses me out. I told him I could recognize that this lady was dealing with some kind of difficulty in her life and that it wouldn't hurt us to try to be patient and understanding.

A little while later, as we were getting ready to leave, I took some cash out of my wallet to leave her a tip. When I did, my son asked me, "Why are you leaving her a tip? She was horrible." After thinking about it for a moment, I told him, "It is not our job to judge. However, it is our job to show God's love to the people that are hurting."

Then, just as we were about to leave, the waitress walked by, and I smiled and said, "Thank you. Have a blessed day." I realized it wouldn't cost me anything to share some kind words.

I may never know if my generosity and kind words had a positive impact on her that day, but I'm sure of the fact that it didn't do any harm. I could have responded to her rudeness with sarcasm, anger, or contempt of my own. What would that have accomplished? It would have stirred up conflict. Why would I wish to ruin my day by engaging in unnecessary conflict? Not to mention the fact that I worked at many restaurants when I was younger, and I know what the servers do to your food if you are rude to them.

So why is it that we have such difficulty using our words to bring peace into our lives? Why are we so inclined to use our words for harm rather than for good?

I've learned that the words we speak can either encourage others or discourage others. Our words, like Jesus' words, can raise the dead. Our words can also cause death.

I know we can do a lot of good with words. Unfortunately, we can also do a lot of harm with our words as well.

Proverbs 12:18 *The words of the reckless pierce like swords, but the tongue of the wise brings healing.*

How many of us are guilty of being reckless with our words? I think we all have at some time in our lives.

I know that being a parent is one of the toughest jobs in the world. I have been blessed with a wonderful child that I know has a fantastic future ahead of him. I can't wait to see all the great things he is destined to do in his life. It makes me so proud, just thinking about all that God has planned for him.

However, children seem to have this particular kind of superpower that is only known to exist within the tiniest of human beings. This superpower, as I'm sure most moms and dads have already witnessed, is the ability to push our buttons so hard that it brings out the worst in us. I'm serious, there is no one in this world I love more than my son, but at the same time, there is no one else on this earth that can make me as mad as he can.

How is it that the ones you love the most are the ones that can push you so far past your limits? They can test your patience as no one else can.

These adorable little children grow up and eventually become one of life's most feared creatures - teenagers. Most parents who have been through the rebellious teenage years of their children's lives can testify that maintaining control over their tongue can prove to be a difficult task. It is hard to remember the scriptures that teach us about our words when you have a teenager testing the limits to see how much they can get away with.

I know that I am guilty of being reckless with my words at times. I share this with you so that you understand that no one is perfect and that we all fall short of the grace of God. I believe the reason I am writing this book is because I need to hear the words I am preaching. I need to remind myself of how our thoughts and our words direct our lives.

I believe the devil sometimes uses the most valuable people in our lives to try to drive negativity out of us. We need to stand firm against the enemy. We need to use God's Word as our sword and shield. If we fill our hearts with His precious Word every day, I believe He will give us the strength to overcome all things, even the teenage years. After all, the Bible says we can do all things through Christ who strengthens us.

Proverbs 12:18 also tells us that our words have the power to heal. I make every effort to use my words to lift others up. I tell my son, "I love you" about a hundred times a day. Well, maybe not a hundred times. It seems like that many. Maybe five or six times a day at most. Not more than that.

Many years ago, when my son was little, God shared with me that He has great plans for my son. It's kind of like what He told us in this scripture:

Jeremiah 29:11

For I know the plans I have for you," declares the LORD, "plans to prosper you and not to harm you, plans to give you hope and a future.

Because I have this knowledge, I choose to use it to lift him up every chance I can. I remind him that even though he may experience difficulties and trials of all kinds, that he does not need to feel discouraged. This is because God knows the plans that He has for him, and they are for his good. I believe that my son is inspired by these faith-filled words that I share with him.

Words can heal almost every wound. How about the words, I'm sorry? These two words are not used as often as they should be. These simple words can change the world. They can heal relationships, and they can destroy resentment, anger, and even regret.

We are all human, and we all make mistakes. We all disagree and argue about various things. We do so with loved ones, people at work, or even with people we hardly know. When we fail to use these two simple words, *I'm sorry*, we end up creating grudges and bad feelings between ourselves and others.

Words can also hurt ourselves just as much as they can hurt those around us. Years ago, when I met my wife, I remember her being a glass half full kind of person, while I had always been a glass half empty type of guy. In the early days of our relationship, I would always hear her say, "Take that back!" This is what I would hear from her when she caught me speaking negatively about a circumstance or situation.

Whenever I had a cold and was coughing, sneezing, and felt miserable, I would go around all day talking about how horrible I felt. I would say things like "I feel like a was run over by a train," or, "I feel like I'm about to die." When I did this, I would hear her remind me that I was giving the devil authority to act on my words by declaring these negative things.

I have heard her over the years tell me a thousand times to "Take that back!" I have listened to it so much that I think it has helped me be a more positive person. Nowadays, I walk around telling her to "Take that back!" when she speaks negativity over her life and her circumstances.

In the past, I have told myself and anyone else that was willing to listen to me, things like, "All I have is bad luck," or, "If it weren't for bad luck, I wouldn't have any luck at all." How many of us are guilty of this one? I know I'm not the only one.

The problem with this type of mindset is that we are declaring this negativity over our lives. Rather than talking about how we feel at the moment, we need to use our words to proclaim God's blessings over our lives. Rather than talking about how nothing good ever happens to us, we should remind ourselves how much God has blessed us.

Seriously, do we realize how truly blessed we are? I'm sure I'm not the only one that heard my mom say to me when I was a child, as I was complaining about how I didn't like what she cooked for dinner, "You are not going anywhere until you finish your dinner. We don't waste food in this house. Do you realize how many people in this world are starving and would be thankful for what you have?"

We have so many things to be thankful for. The food we have on the table is a blessing. No matter if it's Ramen noodles or filet mignon. There are so many people in this world that don't have either one available to them.

Rather than talking about how bad my luck is, I should be talking about how blessed I am. Rather than talking about how nothing ever works out for me, I should talk about how God will work everything out for my good. (Romans 8:28)

Think about how we use our words, and when you do, consider this old saying - *you need to dress for the job you want, not the job you have.* In a literal sense, this phrase means that you wouldn't want to go interview for a bank manager position dressed in sweatpants and a baseball cap. You would want to wear a suit and tie.

What this saying means, metaphorically speaking, is that we need to project what we want in our lives, not what we have.

We can have aches and pains, but if all we do is complain about them and focus all of our thoughts and words on them, those thoughts will consume us and magnify the pain. Why put a spotlight on something as negative as pain? Why magnify it?

What we need to do is use our words to project what we hope our situation to be. We need to declare our healing. We need to declare that we are healthy and strong.

Now I'm not saying that if we remain positive and declare healing over our sickness, that we will be magically healed. I'm not even going to tell you that God will heal you. I am telling you that we each have the power within us to perceive the circumstances whichever way we choose to. We can view a difficulty in our lives negatively and allow it to fill our heart, mind, and soul with fear, anxiety, and worry. Or, we can choose to deal with the difficulties in our lives with an attitude of faith. Doing so will allow the fear, anxiety, and worry to turn into peace, faith, and hope.

Remaining positive in a difficult situation isn't easy. But if we train ourselves to use our words to magnify God, rather than the difficulty, we can change our perspective and see things through His eyes rather than through our own eyes.

When we look at the circumstances through our own eyes, we can see defeat. When we look at things through the eyes of God, we will be able to see things as He sees them. He can see the beginning and the end. We can only see what's in front of us.

He knows things will work out for us in the end. He knows that He will be there for us, to care for us and comfort us. He knows that when our trials and tribulations are over, we will be resting safely in His arms.

When we look through His eyes, we can see how it all ends. It ends with God's arms wrapped around us, like a father hugging his child.

Before we end this chapter, I'd like to discuss how God feels about our words and how we use them.

Ephesians 4:29 *Do not let any unwholesome talk come out of your mouths, but only what is helpful for building others up according to their needs, that it may benefit those who listen.*

God commands us to use our words to bless others. He is very clear about what His will is when it comes to words. This is why gossip is a sin. It usually does nothing but hurt someone else.

Swearing is also a sin. One could argue that a word is just a word and that a swear word is no different than any other word. That is not true. The difference between a swear word and any other word is the intended meaning behind it. Swear words are designed to have a negative connotation attached to them. They are not intended to be used positively.

Not only do we need to consider the words we speak, but also the tone we use when we speak them. Don't be fooled into believing that you speak in a godly manner when you use sarcasm or scream the words out. Just because you use words that are generally non-offensive doesn't mean that you are not offensive.

We need to pay close attention to this next scripture. This is an important one.

Matthew 12:36-37 *But I tell you that everyone will have to give account on the day of judgment for every empty word they have spoken. For by your words you will be acquitted, and by your words you will be condemned."*

I don't know about you, but I'm beginning to feel a little uncomfortable right about now. Reading this verse by itself, apart from other scripture, can instill fear into anyone's soul.

It scares me to think that I will have to give an account to God for the words I have spoken throughout my life. By no means am I innocent when it comes to misusing the power of my words. I don't know how I could ever explain to God why I said some of the things I have said in my life. When I think about the moment I stand before God and give an account, I am reminded of all the arguments I have gotten into with family, friends, and co-workers over the years. So many times, I have chosen words that are not useful for giving life, but rather, for bringing death unto someone.

Just like everyone else, I realize I have not always used my words for good. I struggle with the thought that I am only human, and I make mistakes, and I hope that God will accept this explanation and honor my plea for mercy.

When I think of how I am guilty of gossip and using harsh words in my life, I realize that I can't turn back the hands of time. I understand there is nothing I can do to change the past. However, I do realize that I do have the power to change the present.

Remember when Jesus told the adulterer's accusers, "He who is without sin may cast the first stone."? He then told the women, "Go and sin no more." What Jesus did here was forgive her of her past sins. This scripture is evidence of God's forgiving heart. We must remember not to take advantage of His generosity. Jesus did command the women to *sin no more*.

So, while my past mistakes sometimes haunt me, I can take joy in the fact that I am forgiven and free to start over again each day, with a renewed heart and mind, striving to honor God with my obedience to His word and to go and sin no more.

In this chapter, these scriptures we have discussed and many more that you can find in your Bible are God's instructions on how to use the power of our words to be obedient to his will.

Not only should we use our words wisely in order to please God and avoid hurting others, but also to make our lives better.

Let's discuss this one last scripture before we move on.

1 Peter 3:10

If you want to enjoy life and see many happy days, keep your tongue from speaking evil and your lips from telling lies.

We see that God's desire is to use the gift of our words to provide ourselves with a long and happy life.

Just like most of God's laws, they are not intended to control us. They are designed to protect us. When we disobey God's commandments, we can find ourselves in all kinds of danger. Like any other good father, all He wants for His children is to keep us safe, happy, and blessed.

Chapter Eleven

How to defeat the enemy

In this chapter, we are going to discuss how we can defeat the enemy. We are going to discuss how we can use his *What if* strategy against him.

While we must remember he is a demon of deception, he is in no way a match for God. As long as we choose to prepare ourselves for battle and use God's word as a sword, we can overcome all of life's negative *What ifs*.

As discussed before, Satan's objective is to steal, kill, and destroy. We now know some of the tactics he uses to accomplish those goals. We know that he tries to tempt us into sin. We know that he tries to deceive us into believing that we should follow him instead of God. We also know that he uses fear to try to control us and to steal away our faith.

We know that fear leads us to anxiety and worry. We also know that worry, fear, and anxiety are the opposite of peace, faith, and hope. We understand you can't go up the same time you are going down and that you can't go left the same time you are going right. In the same manner, we cannot have both faith and fear at the same time. We cannot have peace and anxiety at the same time. And we cannot have hope and worry simultaneously. We must choose. We need to use our free will to choose one or the other. We need to decide to trust God and surrender our lives to Him.

I understand this isn't easy. Surrendering to anyone other than ourselves, goes against our nature as human beings. We were born into a world of sin. We naturally desire to yield only to the lusts of the flesh.

Society has done a great job of encouraging this behavior. We are flooded with messages of hate, anger, greed, and self-centeredness. We are taught that it is ok to step on others in order to get what we want. These are some of the things the world teaches. The great news is that we do not belong to this world. We belong to God.

Satan will never give up. He will continue to wreak havoc on our lives as long as we allow him to. He will continue to flood our minds with all kinds of negative *what ifs*. Thoughts like, what if I lose my job and can't pay my bills, or what if I get cancer or some other terminal illness? The negative *what ifs* can be endless.

We need to focus on positive *what-ifs*, like, what if I could trust God for everything? Or, what if God's promises are true?

In chapter six, we talked about how fear can cripple us. Fear can keep us from reaching our goals and fulfilling God's will for our lives.

For example, when the time came for me to write my first book, I didn't know where to begin. I didn't know how to write a book. I had never written anything before. I was afraid to share my life story with the world. I thought, what if it doesn't turn out well? I then thought, what if people don't like it?

The *what ifs* didn't stop there. The flood of *what ifs* continued to pour into my mind. What if people don't believe my story is true? What if no one reads it? I had all these negative what-ifs in my mind trying to stop me from fulfilling God's purpose and plan for my life. If I had listened to all these *what ifs*, I would never have found out that God planted this talent deep within me. I would never have found out that God has called me to glorify Him through the words I write.

All the *what ifs* that I struggled with turned out to be nothing more than the devil's lies. He tried to fill my heart with fear in order to tempt me into giving up. I suppose it could have been because he knew that thousands of people worldwide would read it. He might have known that people would love it. He might have suspected that it could even bring faith to those whose faith was weak and bring hope to the hopeless. He probably was afraid that it might also teach people how to forgive. I suppose if I were him, I wouldn't want me to have written this first book either.

Now, while Satan might try this same strategy again as I'm writing this book, I can be confident that I am doing what God has called me to do. And because of this, I can be convinced that this book will turn out well. I can now ask, what if a thousand people read this book? What if a hundred thousand read this book? What if this book helps people live with more faith, peace, and hope? What if I can help others to overcome fear, worry, and anxiety? What if?

Let's look at this scripture:

Psalm 32:8

I will instruct you and teach you in the way you should go; I will counsel you with my loving eye on you.

There will be plenty of times in life when we are unsure of what path to take. When a difficult decision is presented to us, like when I had to decide whether I should share my life story with the world, we can be sure that God will be with us and that He will guide us. He makes this promise to us in Psalm 32:8.

His promises can reassure us that we don't need to surrender to the enemy's *what ifs*. If we pray and seek Him, and if we are patient enough to listen for His response, He will teach us the way we should go. It's when we do not seek Him that we get lost. It's when we do not listen that we go astray.

All the negative *what ifs* in life are lies. If we trust in God, we will know that there is no weapon formed against us that will prosper (Isaiah 54:17). God tells us in Philippians 4:19 that He will supply all our needs according to His riches in glory through Christ Jesus. In Romans 8:31, we are told that no one can be against us if God is for us. There are countless promises in the Bible about God's faithfulness.

When we look at David and Goliath's story, we can only imagine how David's life would have turned out if he had surrendered to all of the devil's negative *what ifs*.

I know the Bible doesn't record it, but I can imagine that David might have faced many *what ifs*. Like, what if I'm not good enough to defeat the giant? What if I'm not strong enough? What if I don't win? What if I die? David could easily have surrendered to all these negative *what ifs*. After all, he was just a young shepherd boy. David didn't have the experience, skill, or training to defeat a giant. He could have decided to run away and hide. David could have chosen to walk away from the purpose and plan that God had for his life. Can you imagine if he did this? Would he have gone on to become king? Would he have gone on to live the life that God had planned for him?

What about you? Is there an area of your life that you are not growing in because you all allowing all the negative *what ifs* to fill your heart with fear?

I can tell you about another time in my life when Satan tried relentlessly to stop me from living God's plan for my life. Years ago, when I was 25 years old, I had the desire in my heart to start a business. At the time, I didn't have much money. I certainly didn't have enough experience to start my own business. The company I wanted to start required an initial investment of $75,000. This would cover the initial franchise fee and operating expenses for the first year. At the time, I had saved $12,500 from working hard over the prior ten years of my life. This was not nearly enough to have a reasonable chance of being successful. I knew that if I decided to do this, I would be facing an uphill battle.

When I was planning on starting this business, I had just found out I was going to become a dad. I felt a lot of pressure to find a way to provide the best life possible for my son. I knew if I didn't at least try, that there would be no way to give him the life he deserves.

While I struggled to decide whether or not I should start this business, I heard the enemy's *what ifs* float through my mind. I remember thinking, what if this business fails and I lose everything? What if the bank doesn't approve my loan request? What if I start this business and can't find the right employees to staff my office? What if, after my best marketing efforts are made, no one comes into my office to have their taxes prepared by my company? What if I get ill and can't work? What if?

I was bombarded by all these *what ifs* that told me I shouldn't do it. The *what ifs* told me that it couldn't be done. The *what ifs* told me I was too young. The *what ifs* told me that the more experienced competitors would crush my attempt to be successful. The *what ifs* told me to surrender. They told me to surrender to the fear. They told me to give in to the anxiousness and worry.

While I could have chosen to surrender to these *what ifs*, I decided to focus on faith-filled *what ifs* instead. I decided to think, what if I can succeed?

What if my hard work pays off? What if, after opening my first office, I open several others? What if I do my best and trust God for the rest? What if?

While facing one of the scariest decisions of my life, I decided to pray and seek God's wisdom. I waited patiently to hear His word. I had gone back and forth for months, trying to figure out what God's plan was for my life.

After struggling to overcome the negative *what ifs* and using the positive *what ifs* to balance out the pros and cons, I realized that moving forward would indeed be difficult, but that it would not be impossible. I realized I would have to work much harder than I had ever worked before. I also knew that it would require sacrifice.

While I knew the odds of being successful were not in my favor, I also knew that the one who is for me is greater than anyone that is against me.

So, what did I do? I started the business. I borrowed tens of thousands of dollars on my credit cards. I went deep into debt, worked hard, and several years later, God blessed me with success.

Now I know I'm not the only one who struggles with negative *what ifs*. I can tell you about a person I know that surrenders to the negative *what ifs* frequently. This person is continually taking these negative *what ifs* and proclaiming them as if they are guaranteed to happen. All I hear from them are things like, "You better not go to the beach, because if you do, you are going to get flesh-eating bacteria," or,

"You shouldn't spend too much time in the sun. You are going to get skin cancer." When I hear these things, my spirit is instantly awakened. I immediately recognize the source of this negativity. I try to correct this person, but the pattern of negativity seems to continue.

I suppose I should continue to pray for them and give them an autographed copy of this book when it's finished.

When the Bible tells us to call things that are not, as though they already are, it doesn't mean that we are to go around talking about all the negative things we worry about and declare that they are going to happen. It means that we are supposed to declare that the promises of God are going to happen. It means that we are to proclaim blessings over our lives.

The Bible teaches us to use faith to declare godly things. In the gospel of Matthew, the woman who had a problem with bleeding for twelve years said, "If I can just touch his robe, then I will be healed." She had the faith to declare it. When she declared it and then touched His robe, she was healed.

I'm not telling you to go around declaring things like, "Someday I'm going to win the lottery," or anything like that. All I'm telling you is that if you live with faith, believing for God's best, that you will have more peace in your life.

I want to share with you this recipe that I have written in my heart. These are some of the ingredients that I use in my life to overcome the enemy's *what ifs*.

1. Build and maintain a relationship with God through prayer, church, and the study of His Word.
2. Choose to trust God when everything else around you tells you that you shouldn't.
3. When things get tough, remember there will be better times ahead, whether in this life or the next.
4. Know that you have authority over your circumstances. Remember that God is in control, not the devil.
5. Use your thoughts to overcome the enemy. Focus your mind on all that is good and pure.
6. Use your words to defeat the devil. Speak to your problems. Tell them who is in charge.

These are just some of the things we can do to live a life filled with positive *what ifs*, as well as faith, hope, and peace.

Before we finish talking about how to overcome the tactics of the enemy, we have to take a look at this scripture:

Philippians 4:6-7

"Do not be anxious about anything, but in every situation, by prayer and petition, with thanksgiving, present your requests to God. And the peace of God, which transcends all understanding, will guard your hearts and your minds in Christ Jesus."

In this scripture, Paul tells us that we do not need to be anxious about anything. He instructs us what to do when worry, fear, and anxiety begin to creep up on us. He says that we are to pray with a thankful heart, presenting all of our requests to God. We are to do this when we hear those *what ifs* the devil whispers in our ears. We need to stop him dead in his tracks. When we do, Paul tells us that the peace of God will guard our hearts and our minds. God's peace transcends all understanding. His peace is and will always be greater than any *What if*.

The End.

Hi. My name is John Stone. I want to thank you for reading this book. I hope you enjoyed it. If you did, please tell your friends and family about it, and help me share the gospel with the world.

You can also go to my website to learn about my three other books, **The Promise**, **Words of Wisdom**, and **High School Journal**. Here is a brief description of each of these books:

The Promise
A Story of Faith, Love, and Forgiveness.

This book is based on a true story that describes the trials and tribulations a father must face as he fights to protect his son from his son's abusive biological mother.

This story will touch the deepest part of your soul and make you feel as though you are living the story, rather than just reading it.

Here is the official description of the book:

This love story begins with plenty of passion and romance, just as most other love stories do. However, when John and Tiffany's relationship ends, chaos quickly emerges. Their infant son gets caught in the middle as he is ruthlessly kidnapped from his father and then endures years of abuse.

John is then forced to endure years of stalking, harassment, threats, false accusations, and even an attempt on his life. He endures all of this, all for the love of his son.

In this book, which is based on a dramatic true story, a father must face countless challenges when his son's mother, who has Borderline Personality Disorder, stops at nothing in her attempt to dismantle his life. Little does she know that God has promised this young father that He would someday bring his son back home to him.

Accompany the author as he takes you through his journey of faith is this heartwarming and dramatic autobiography. Feel the love that he has for his son as he risks his life and his freedom to be with him. Accompany John Stone to the end of his journey, where God's promise is fulfilled and forgiveness reigns.

Words of Wisdom

This book is a collection of teachings based upon various biblical principles. It will strengthen your relationship with God and draw you closer to Him. The teachings contained within these pages will help you understand how to get through all of life's difficulties and overcome all of life's challenges.

High School Journal

High School Journal is the first in a series of romance novels that follows the life of a teenage girl named Paige, as she struggles through life's difficulties while beginning her journey through high school.

You can purchase a copy of **The Promise, High School Journal and Words Of Wisdom** by visiting my website at: **www.Johnstonebooks.com**

Follow me on Facebook and Instagram to learn more about me and my upcoming books.

Email me at
Contact@Johnstonebooks.com

Visit my website at
www.JohnStoneBooks.com

Follow me on Facebook at
www.Facebook.com/JohnStoneBooks

Follow me on Instagram at
www.Instagram.com/john.stone.author

Made in the USA
Middletown, DE
05 July 2024

56865914R00068